HOW SHE FOUND HER ROAR!

L. M. HERNANDEZ

Trilogy Christian Publishers
A Wholly Owned Subsidiary of Trinity Broadcasting Network
2442 Michelle Drive
Tustin, CA 92780
Copyright © 2024 by L.M. Hernandez
Scripture quotations marked AMP are taken from the Amplified® Bible (AMP), Copyright © 2015 by The Lockman Foundation. Used by permission. www.Lockman.org. Scripture quotations marked ASV are taken from the American Standard Version. Public domain. Scripture quotations marked ESV are taken from the ESV® Bible (The Holy Bible, English Standard Version®), copyright © 2001 by Crossway Bibles, a publishing ministry of Good News Publishers. Used by permission. All rights reserved. Scripture quotations marked MEV are taken from the Modern English Version. Copyright © 2014 by Military Bible Association. Used by permission. All rights reserved. Scripture quotations marked NIV are taken from the Holy Bible, New International Version®, NIV®. Copyright © 1973, 1978, 1984, 2011 by Biblica, Inc.TM Used by permission of Zondervan. All rights reserved worldwide. www.zondervan.com. The "NIV" and "New International Version" are trademarks registered in the United States Patent and Trademark Office by Biblica, Inc.TM Scriptures marked NKJV are taken from the New King James Version®. Copyright © 1982 by Thomas Nelson. Used by permission. All rights reserved.
All rights reserved, including the right to reproduce this book or portions thereof in any form whatsoever.
For information, address Trilogy Christian Publishing
Rights Department, 2442 Michelle Drive, Tustin, Ca 92780.
Trilogy Christian Publishing/TBN and colophon are trademarks of Trinity Broadcasting Network.
For information about special discounts for bulk purchases, please contact Trilogy Christian Publishing.
Trilogy Disclaimer: The views and content expressed in this book are those of the author and may not necessarily reflect the views and doctrine of Trilogy Christian Publishing or the Trinity Broadcasting Network.
10 9 8 7 6 5 4 3 2 1
Library of Congress Cataloging-in-Publication Data is available.
ISBN 979-8-89041-615-5
ISBN 979-8-89041-616-2 (ebook)

ENDORSEMENTS

Lisa Hernandez is the equivalent of a female spiritual general teaching in the War College of the Armed Forces. She has a supernatural anointing to discern, see, facilitate, and empower the body of Christ, particularly women, to walk into their rank and commission as warrior women and use their voices in every sphere with spiritual authority through prophetic prayer. Her narrative is resplendent with biblical texts supporting her view that the ROAR of God is deep inside each of us and only needs to be discovered and mentored in order for us to see cultures shift.

If you feel the stirring of God to "war with your ROAR," I highly recommend this book as a primer for those who are called to rise as warrior princes and princesses!

—Cathy Heiliger
Co-Founder/President Flourish Now, LLC
Certified Life Coach and Stress Consultant
http://www.cathyheiliger.com
Amazon Bestselling Author of *Encounters of the Heart, There's More to the Story Than Meets the Eye, Book Two*
https://amzn.to/2Q513QS

I have known Lisa for twenty years. I have also had the honor of serving with Lisa for the past fifteen years in our church, both in small group ministry and outreach ministry. We have been on mission trips together and have partnered in our ministry at a placement for troubled youth for the past ten years. Lisa was a small group leader for several years and has poured her time, energy, and God-given gifts into discipling other women to grow closer to the Lord. She served on our prayer team and is a member of my small group, where she faithfully encourages our women to grow in God.

I have seen Lisa and her family go through extremely difficult challenges in the years that I have known her, and she has been a shining example of one who stands firm in her faith and has chosen to surrender all to God as she continues to trust Him for deliverance from the fiery trials that she has endured. She has allowed God to use those experiences to refine her and prepare her for the assignments He has prepared for her now and in the future.

I can say with confidence that Lisa is a wonderful addition to the authors who contribute to the faith by their witness. I know that many would be blessed and inspired by her words.

—Linda Brown

BOOK OVERVIEW

Most of us who read the Bible know that Jesus is referred to as "The Lion of the tribe of Judah." But, did you know that there are many places in the Old Testament where Jesus, The Lion of the tribe of Judah, inhabits the shout of His people? *How She Found Her ROAR* is a study about the many times throughout the Bible that the Lord gave His *ROAR* to His beloved to conquer the enemies of Israel and bring freedom to His chosen people—how He has given this same gift to His beloved bride to bring forth in us, His overcoming power to make us more than conquerors! Within this book, we will explore the different forms that this *ROAR* can manifest through His bride to accomplish His will in defeating the enemy of our soul! This book is primarily meant to inspire the women of God from every tribe, tongue, and nation to step into their true identity in Christ and learn to identify their own version of the *ROAR* of the Lion of Judah. This is a clarion call to women of God and their husbands to come forward in the battle formation and step up to the front lines to take their proper place in the kingdom, save our families, take back our neighborhoods and schools, and strengthen our church by learning basic battle strategies and skills. This book includes several prophetic words that the Lord has released through His servant, the author, and is meant to stir your spirit and stoke the holy fire of God within you!

The author uses her background as a black belt, from more than twenty-five years of experience in martial arts as an instructor, including ten years of competition in karate.

L. M. Hernandez is a wife of thirty-six years and a mother and grandmother. She encourages and leads by example, having endured many valleys and wilderness times where the Lord taught her how to use her background in martial arts to glean strategies, tactical techniques, and situational awareness in the spirit realm from her experience, including an explanation of weapons and how to apply them to the spiritual realm that is at work in us and around us at all times.

Find your *ROAR* within the pages of the Bible through the study of this book!

TABLE OF CONTENTS

AN OPEN VISION, SPRING, 2017:

THE LIONESSES' ROAR IS BEING RESTORED

This is the trustworthy word of the Lord of Hosts, and this is what He says, "Do not weep, daughters of Zion. The Lion of the tribe of Judah, the Root of David, has triumphed!"

He is able to open the scroll and its seven seals. He has come to restore the voice of His lionesses. Just as when Joshua marched around the city of Jericho following the Lord's every instruction, and at the last moment, the commander of the army of the Lord told the people to *shout*, for He had delivered Jericho and its fighting men and king into Joshua's hands. Joshua was told by the Great I Am not to give a war cry, raise their voices, or even say a word until the day He told them to *shout*.

Then, *shout*! Because that is what he was told.

At the seventh time around the city, when the priests sounded the trumpets' blast, Joshua, according to the Word of the Lord of Hosts, commanded the people to *shout*!

When all the people shouted, the wall collapsed. So, every man charged right in and took the city. For when the people shouted, it was no ordinary war cry. It was a Holy Spirit-filled *ROAR*! The Lion of Zion used His voice through His peoples' shout against the enemy, and the enemy could no longer stand or hold onto their ground, so much so that the shockwave that went out from the heaven-filled shouts of God's people made the stronghold of the enemy completely collapse.

The Lord of Hosts, The Lion of the tribe of Judah, has raised up in this generation a remnant of women all over the world who will be so Spirit-filled that they will carry this *ROAR* of the Holy Spirit. Like a lioness, who dares rouse her?

The Lord our God is with us. The shout of the King is among us. At His word, when the time is right, He will instruct us on how to *ROAR* with the power and authority of the Holy Spirit!

He shall bring down the strongholds that are holding our loved ones captive, and spiritual fighting men and their demonic princes who have built up the fortresses will be brought down and utterly destroyed.

The armies of the Lord will rush into these once-fortified places and take these loved ones' lives back form destruction.

The Lord wants to specifically do this using the lionesses who have known what suffering is, for they have been forged by the fire in the furnace of refinement, and they are being given new armor and new names in the Spirit realm, along with new mantles being released.

So, daughters, get your sword sharpened and ask the Holy Spirit to teach you how and when to use your lioness of Zion *ROAR*! Take back your homes, and the atmosphere around you will change, and wall after wall will begin to fall as you begin to use your heavenly *ROAR*!

Not only in our homes but also in our spheres of influence, our cities, workplaces, churches, our children's schools, and everywhere we go, we will come out from among those that the enemy has been holding back, and our heavenly names will be known by the enemy before we enter into our spheres of influence. When the enemy sees the daughters, brides, and those we have brought with us out of captivity—those whom the *ROAR* of the Lord has set free—they will see us coming from afar off, and the enemy will surrender!

It is time to take back the spiritual dominion that Christ died in order to bring under His feet and under ours.

See scripture references here: Matthew 22:44, Romans 16:20, 1 Corinthians 15:27, Ephesians 1:22, Hebrews 2:28.

"And God placed all things under His feet and appointed Him to be head over everything for the church, which is His body, the fullness of Him who fills everything in every way" (Ephesians 1:22–23, NIV).

Five times, this verse or a version of it appears in Scripture.

Five is the number identified with God's grace. Aren't we, as His daughters, the embodiment of His beauty and His grace? If you agree, shout *amen*!

CHAPTER 1:
ROAR!

What does it mean to *ROAR*? It is a full, deep, prolonged cry uttered by a lion. This is the description found in Webster's Dictionary.

A lion can ROAR as loud as 114 decibels, about 25 times louder than a gas-powered lawn mower. The cats are also aided by the strength of their vocal folds, which can withstand stretching and shearing. As air moves past them, the folds vibrate. Lions ROAR to communicate between members of the same pride or coalition and to advertise territory.

Why on earth would I want to *ROAR*?

In April 2017, I was in my quiet time with the Lord when I suddenly felt the Holy Spirit come upon me. This was not the first time I had received a word from Him. He has often petitioned me to pray for nations and leaders near and far. But this word was different. It was specifically for God's women. As I began to write what I was hearing in this open vision, He told me that we, as women, had lost our ROAR. He, who is faithful, wanted to restore the lionesses' ROAR.

Here is where you are probably thinking: *Why me?* I said the same thing to Him in the spirit. Then, He reminded me of my earthly warrior status. I am a black belt, and I have trained in karate, kickboxing, hand-to-hand combat, and weapons for more than two decades. I was once a fierce competitor. But when I ran after the Lord with everything that I am, I let go of all of that and went to work with troubled youth.

When I was an instructor, I taught many self-defense classes to women. One of the things I taught them, in fact, one of the first things I taught them, was the ki (the spirit cry). In China, it is called chi. In Japan, it is called ki. Both reference the use of a loud, prolonged cry uttered from deep in the gut. It has been shown that shouting as you fight can increase your intensity. It releases endorphins and is a call to the body that we are under attack! Our own mighty armed forces also learn the "spirit cry" in their training.

When I taught women to ki, I often would go through the explanation that I just gave to you. However, I would add this, "The Christian would call this inner spirit—*the Holy Spirit*." Even then, I knew that the true cry of the warrior for God was the ROAR! Look again at the definition. "A full, deep, prolonged cry uttered by a lion." But it is not only my ROAR that the Lord wanted me to rediscover. He wanted me to use His voice of authority, His "ROAR"!

As an instructor or sensei, I had the opportunity to work with women who had been in hidden shelters because of the abuse that they and their children had suffered. I can never forget how beaten down the ladies looked at the start of the class. I would get them all fired up by giving them a "pep talk," and then I would teach them how to use their voice. They were shy at first, but I would pace back and forth in front of them, urging them to *shout* louder, louder! Then, I would see the look in their eyes change from weary to alive! They stood up straighter and opened their mouths wider, and then they would *ROAR*! Of course, I taught the ladies some basic self-defense moves that could help them break the grip of their attacker and disable them. But it all started with the spirit cry. I loved seeing the look on the children's faces as they saw their mothers regain their voices. They were brimming with admiration for them. What a beautiful thing to behold, praise God!

God's Word is full of examples of holy fighters bellowing this ROAR of the Lion of the tribe of Judah.

"Then one of the elders said to me, 'Do not weep! See, the Lion of the tribe of Judah, the root of David, has triumphed. He is able to open the scroll and its seven seals'" (Revelation 5:5, NIV).

We see that Christ is referred to as "the Lion of the tribe of Judah."

He is the true King from the lineage of David. He is Lord of heaven and earth. There is power in using the names of God when we pray. We like to pray in the name of Jesus to the Father. This is how we should pray. Maybe we should also add praying in the name of Jesus, the Lion of the tribe of Judah, the Lamb that was slain but is alive. He is the one who holds the keys to the seven seals! He holds the keys to our deliverance from the enemy! Here it is again in Genesis:

Judah, your brothers will praise you;
your hand will be on the neck of your enemies;
your fathers' sons will bow down to you.
You are a lion's cub, Judah;
you return from the prey, my son.
Like a lion, he crouches and lies down,
like a lioness—who dares to rouse him?
The scepter will not depart from Judah,
nor the ruler's staff from between his feet,
until he to whom it belongs shall come
And the obedience of the nations shall be his.

Genesis 49:8–10 (NIV)

What should we learn from the Lion of the tribe of Judah?

Each of the twelve sons of Israel (Jacob) received a blessing from their father just before his death. The twelve sons were the origin of the twelve tribes of Israel, and the blessing spoken over each of them contained prophetic information about the future of the tribe. In the case of the tribe of Judah, Jacob prophesied over Judah's bloodline.

In verse 8, Jacob prophesies that Judah's brothers would praise him. The name Judah means praise. His mother named him Judah because she was so filled with praise to God for him. Judah was comparable to a young lion because of his strength, courage, and vitality and to a mature lion in that the line of Judah contained those of national prominence and kinship, including David and Solomon, and eventually Jesus, King of kings. "The scepter not departing from his hand until He comes to whom it belongs" is a messianic prophecy. "Your hand will be on the neck of your enemies."

Throughout history, great kings who defeated their foes would gather the enemy kings and their men, and the victorious king would step on the necks of his enemies in front of all of the people gathered. We see this example in Joshua Chapter 10:24–26:

> *When they had brought these kings to Joshua, he summoned all the men of Israel and said to the army commanders who had come with him, "Come here and put your feet on the necks of these kings." So, they came forward and placed their feet on their necks.*
>
> *Joshua said to them, "Do not be afraid; do not be discouraged. Be strong and courageous. This is what the LORD will do to*

all the enemies you are going to fight." Then Joshua put the kings to death and exposed their bodies on five poles and they were left hanging on the poles until evening.

Joshua 10:24–26 (NIV)

It is a rather gruesome picture of what the Lord will do for His people against their enemies. This applies to the spiritual fighting men and their kings.

There are many examples of the Lord fighting for His people.

The word "Shiloh" refers to the Messiah. "Shiloh" translates roughly as "a place of worship and rest." Verses 11–12 refer to the abundance of riches that would belong to the tribe of Judah. This applies to the spiritual riches in Christ that flow from the throne in heaven to those who have been grafted into the family tree, as stated in Romans 11:11–24 and John 15:1–17. We are grafted into the lineage of the Lion of the tribe of Judah. None other than King Jesus! This is what He says about His descendants:

No misfortune is seen in Jacob. No misery observed in Israel. The LORD their God is with them; the shout of the King is among them.

God brought them out of Egypt they have the strength of a wild ox.

There is no divination against Jacob.

No evil omens against Israel.

> *It will be said of Jacob and of Israel, "See what God has done!"*
>
> *The people rise like a lioness, they rouse themselves like a lion; that does not rest until it devours its prey, and drinks the blood of its victims.*
>
> **Numbers 23:21–24 (NIV)**

Where does the *ROAR* fit into this inheritance?

Look again at the verses above. Did you catch it? "The *shout* of the King is among them."

The Lord led me to several battles in the Old Testament where God commanded the people to shout! One battle, in particular, stood out for me. You are probably familiar with the battle I speak of. It is most certainly considered one of Joshua's most famous battles.

I would like for you to look at it with fresh insight from the Holy Spirit; before we go any further, let's pause; pray with me.

Lord Jesus, the Lion of the tribe of Judah. How great is Your glory! Adonai, we kneel before Your throne and ask You to now open our spiritual eyes to what we have not seen. Show us, Lord. Open our spiritual ears to what we have not yet perceived. Show us, Lord. In Jesus's mighty name, we pray, amen!

Let's turn to Joshua, where one of the most epic battles of all time took place: the battle for Jericho (Joshua 3:5).

One of the first things Joshua told the people of Israel to do was to consecrate themselves, "Consecrate yourselves, for tomorrow, the Lord will do amazing things among you" (Joshua 3:5, NIV).

Before the people of Israel could go out into battle, they had to make sure that they were spiritually in the right standing with the Lord of Hosts. It is always wise to do a heart check before we run into battle.

I have found that it is good for me to sit quietly at His feet and confess (Psalm 139). I ask Him to reveal anything in me that is in agreement with the enemy. I ask Him to search me, test me, and reveal any offense I am holding against anyone and make in me a clean heart. I then strap on and fasten my armor.

> *Finally, be strong in the Lord and in his might and power. Put on the full armor of God, so that you can take your stand against the devil's schemes. For our struggle is not against flesh and blood, but against the rulers, against the authorities, against the powers of this dark world and against the spiritual forces of evil in the heavenly realms. Therefore, put on the full armor of God, so that when the day of evil comes, you may be able to stand your ground, and after you have done everything, to stand. Stand firm then, with the belt of truth buckled around your waist, with the breastplate of righteousness in place, and with your feet fitted with the readiness that*

> *comes from the gospel of peace. In addition to all this, take up the shield of faith, with which you can extinguish all the flaming arrows of the evil one. Take the helmet of salvation and the sword of the spirit, which is the word of God. And pray in the Spirit on all occasions with all kinds of prayers and requests. With this in mind, be alert and always keep on praying for all of the Lord's people. Pray also for me, that whenever I speak, words may be given me so that I will fearlessly make known the mystery of the gospel, for which I am an ambassador in chains. Pray that I may declare it fearlessly, as I should.*
>
> **Ephesians 6:10–20 (NIV)**

In karate, I learned to wield the katana. But before I could take up my sword, I had to prepare my mind and spirit. The first thing I would do is put on my gi. You could call this my under armor. Next, I would pull on the hakama. A hakama is a style of trousers that is worn over your gi pants. They are very wide in the leg and are helpful in concealing the movements of the feet and legs.

There was an elaborate method used to tie the hakama to hold it firmly in place.

You could say that it was my buckler of truth. I would then take my katana in its saya (covering) and slide it delicately into place on my left side.

I would sit on my knees and then pull the katana, still in

the saya, and present it in a bow, placing my face down with my forehead touching the floor before my master instructor. My arms outstretched with the sword in my palms, facing up toward my instructor. He would then give me the head nod that indicated that it was okay for me to rise up, take up my sword, and begin the battle with the invisible forces that I would be fighting. This is known as kata, meaning to fight an imaginary or invisible opponent. There are several spiritual principles at play here.

Putting on my gi was like putting on *the mind of Christ*. The gi is meant to represent that I am ready for instruction from my instructor. I would never enter the dojo without being properly outfitted. It would be an insult to my master instructor, and it would show that I was prideful and lacked respect.

I would not enter into the presence of the Lord without a healthy fear of the righteousness and holiness of Him who sits on the throne. I need to put on the mind of Christ and humble myself in His mighty presence.

To have the mind of Christ means to look at life from our Savior's point of view, having His values and desires in mind.

"For who has known the mind of the Lord as to instruct Him? But we have the mind of Christ" (1 Corinthians 2:16, NIV).

Putting on my hakama is like putting on my *buckler of truth*. The belt of truth is the first part of the spiritual armor listed because without truth, we are lost, and we can be overpowered by the lies of the devil. The truth is rooted in understanding our identity in Christ. We, as daughters of God, must know that we are who He says we are in Him.

> *As the Father has loved me, so have I loved you. Now remain in my love. If you keep my commands, you will remain in my love, just as I have kept my Father's commands and remain in His love. I have told you this so that my joy will be in you and that your joy may be complete. My command is this: Love each other as I have loved you.*
>
> **John 15:9–12 (NIV)**

I recommend reading all of John 15 and all other scriptures that define our identity in Christ Jesus. Only when we know our identity in Him can we wear His armor and wield His weapons of warfare.

The breastplate of righteousness is part of the process we talked about earlier in this chapter. Psalm 139:23–24 (NIV) states, "Search me God and know my heart; test me and know my anxious thoughts. See if there is any offensive way in me, and lead me in the way everlasting." I am not saying that we did not receive the gift of righteousness in Christ when we became a new creation; I am saying in order to walk in it, we need to stay clean. Any thought that we give allowance to can take root in our hearts, whether good or evil.

> *For if by the trespass of the one man, death reigned through that one man, how*

> *much more will those who receive God's abundant provision of grace and of the gift of righteousness reign in life through the one man, Jesus Christ!*
>
> *Consequently, just as one trespass resulted in condemnation for all people, so also one righteous act resulted in justification and life for all people.*
>
> **Romans 5:17–18 (NIV)**

The shoes of the gospel must be strapped firmly in place so that we can stand firm without slipping on the rock that is our firm foundation. We cannot stand firm on the rock, even though it does not move, if we do not have an understanding that our shoes must be firmly on our feet. And we need to have a nonslip grip on our reasons why we choose to follow Jesus. We must be sure of the hope we confess in Him as we share the good news with others.

"Since you are my rock and my fortress, for the sake of your name lead and guide me" (Psalm 31:3, NIV).

"Truly He is my rock and my salvation; He is my fortress; I will not be shaken" (Psalm 62:6, NIV).

"Fear the LORD your God and serve Him. Hold fast to Him and take your oaths in His name" (Deuteronomy 10:20, NIV).

"Let us hold fast the profession of our faith without wavering, for He who promised is faithful" (Hebrews

10:23, NIV).

We can also apply Hebrews 10:23 to the *shield of faith.* Faith in Jesus enables us to bear up under very difficult circumstances without letting the enemy darts of fire come through our force field of faith.

The helmet of salvation must protect our head and neck from the blows of the evil one. He will stop at nothing except the word of our testimony of who we are in Christ. We must never let him plant negative thoughts and emotions in our minds. This is where he is particularly crafty. He whispers thoughts in our spiritual ears. He may whisper thoughts of offense, thoughts of unworthiness, or thoughts that are partial truths wrapped in a lie. It is up to us to stay frosty and vigilant over what we let into our senses. They represent doors and gates. The enemy is very tricky. He will come at you through your earthly senses in order to corrupt your spiritual senses. Seeing, hearing, smelling, tasting, touching—all of these senses are at risk. Also, when we became believers and followers of Jesus Christ, we gained the spiritual sense of knowing.

Know-ing:

1. Showing or suggesting that one has knowledge or awareness that is known to only a few people.
2. Done in full awareness or consciousness of God's presence and will.

Always put on the helmet of salvation to guard your mind.

> *Now the serpent was more crafty than any of the wild animals the LORD God had made. He said to the woman, "Did God really say, 'You must not eat from any tree of the garden'?"*
>
> *The woman said, "We may eat fruit from the trees in the garden, but God did say, 'You must not eat fruit from the tree that is in the middle of the garden, and you must not touch it, or you will die."*
>
> *"You will not certainly die," said the serpent to the woman.*
>
> **Genesis 3:1–4 (NIV)**

"I am afraid that just as Eve was deceived by the serpent's cunning, your minds may somehow be led astray from your sincere and pure devotion to Christ" (2 Corinthians 11:3, NIV).

Guard your doors and gates.

The prayer shield of faith is essential in extinguishing the fiery darts of the enemy. The Bible says we have all been given a measure of faith. We must flex our faith in order that it may grow. In growing our faith, our small shield can become a virtual force field that can wrap around us and our families so that we can withstand the onslaught of the enemy army.

Hebrews 11 is known as the "hall of faith." The entire chapter is full of the children of God, whom the Father Himself counted as righteous because of their great faith.

"Now faith is confidence in what we hope for and assurance about what we do not see" (Hebrews 11:1, NIV).

"You see that a person is considered righteous by what they do and not by faith alone" (James 2:24, NIV).

Of course, we know that the sword of the Spirit is the Word of God.

Hebrews 4:12 (NIV) states, " For the word of God is living and active, Sharper than any two-edged sword, it penetrates even to dividing soul and spirit, joint and bone, judging the thoughts and feelings of the heart."

The sword of the Spirit is my chosen weapon. My master, Jesus of Nazareth, has taught me to wield it well. I still have so much to learn, but I am confident in Him, who goes before me and stands behind me.

The first chapter of John begins, "In the beginning was the Word, and the Word was with God. He was with God in the beginning. Through Him all things were made; without Him nothing was made that has been made" (John 1:1–3, NIV).

It is important to note that Hebrews 4:12 states that both the written and living Word (Jesus) are "living and active."

Samurai were bound to their master, usually an emperor or a governor of a province. The word "samurai" means "to serve." Does that sound familiar? You are not a samurai without a ruler to serve. I serve King Jesus. Before I go into battle, I put on my armor, present my sword to the King of kings, and wait for the moment that He gives me the nod to take up my sword and stand firm.

There is always stillness before the ROAR of the battle cry. The air feels alive, and the mind is fully awake.

One day, as I was walking through the farm on which I work, as is my habit, I was observing God in the natural world around me. As I was rounding the corner to the farm gate that I lock every night, I suddenly stopped in my tracks. I remained perfectly still. I am not sure why I stopped. But I felt compelled to do so. There I stood, and then I realized that everything seemed to be still. Even the breeze that cuts through the lower north part of the farm was uncharacteristically still. I remember speaking out loud, "Lord, what is this that I am experiencing? This stillness, Lord, what does it mean?" Immediately, I heard these words in my spirit, "It is the deep breath before the plunge." I knew these words well.

You see, I am a movie nerd. God knows this. He likes to speak to His children in their love language—in ways that they will understand. So, oftentimes, He uses humor or poignant moments from movies that I love to speak to my spirit. He knows I have a wide-eyed sense of adventure.

I hurried back to my office, and I googled the phrase "The deep breath before the plunge." In The Lord of The Rings Trilogy's *The Return of The King*, there is a scene set high at the top of a mountain, overlooking the precipice of the castle Gondor. Gandalf, the great white wizard, and Pippin, the humble but curious hobbit from the shire, are looking out into the great expanse before them when Pippin feels uneasy; he continues staring outward and says to Gandalf, "It's so quiet." Gandalf, still looking straight ahead, says to Pippin, "It is the deep breath before the plunge."

My heart is prepared.

My mind is at peace.

My armor is in place.

My spirit stands firmly planted on the rock of my salvation.

And I have applied the blood of the Lamb to my lintel and door posts by my confession of faith in Jesus for the forgiveness of my sins.

I am justified, just as if I'd never sinned.

I am ready for battle.

The air is still; not a sound is uttered. I await my master's command.

It is, indeed, the deep breath before the plunge.

OPEN VISION: 10:00 A.M., TUESDAY, MAY 16, 2017

I AM THE ANCIENT OF DAYS

As I kneeled before the Lord in my prayer time, the Holy Spirit came on me, and I received the gift of tongues. The words began to flow so fast that I couldn't keep up with my breaths in between words. Before me, a window view of heaven opened up, and I saw a scroll. On the scroll was heavenly writing in what appeared to be gold. I began reading the scroll out loud in tongues—my eyes moved rapidly back and forth and up, down, and across what was written on the scroll. As I was reading aloud in tongues, I asked the Lord in my heart, "What is this scroll?" This went on for about twenty minutes.

I suddenly opened my eyes and sat silently on the floor for about two minutes. I guess I was a little stunned. Then I said to the Lord, "Do You want me to write it down?"

I heard "yes" in my spirit.

So, in obedience, I wrote down what I had witnessed. This is what flowed from the pen in my hand that day:

I Am the Ancient of Days.
I Am the Lion of the tribe of Judah.

I Am coming on the clouds. The horn has been blown, and the shouts have been heard. Your salvation is here. Your Kinsman Redeemer is here. Now is the time of the open heaven. I have placed My warrior angels in position to fight for you.

Shout, O Israel! Shout, O bride! Sing and break forth in song. Like Deborah and Miriam, go out before the enemy and shout My praises! My glory is upon you, O Israel, O beloved bride! You cannot lose! I have the keys to death and hades. Fear not! For I Am is with you! March around your enemies, and on the seventh time, blow your horn, summoning My warriors. Surely, I say, I will send them in by My ROAR! I have taken up javelin and sword and shield! I am ready to break forth!

Here I come! My coming has felt long to My bride.

Some have grown weary and are just about to give up.

But your battle is already won! So, sing praises!

Play the instruments and wave My banner!

Go out before your enemies and partake of the feast of My blood and My body, which was given for you!

Watch as the enemy is destroyed before your spiritual eyes. Then, My glory will manifest in the natural, and you will see a breakthrough on every side that has been held back by My enemies!

Here I come! The God of angel armies! For I Am and always have been, and always will be, victorious! I sit on the throne, and you will be welcome with Me there. You will receive a hero's welcome.

You will receive the spoils of war, which the enemy has stolen from you! All will be repaid in double!

I am the Lord! I am faithful! This is My Word, which is the truth! Receive it!

Notice in the word I received that Jesus seems to be speaking to women. He mentions Deborah and Miriam. He referred to Himself as the Lion of the tribe of Judah, "I will send them in by My ROAR!"

CHAPTER 2:

TAKE UP YOUR CROSS DAILY AND FOLLOW ME

Now that we have prepared ourselves to the uttermost, we can take up our position in the battle formation. In Joshua Chapter 12, we see the long list of kings that Joshua defeated by God's command. Verses 9 through 24 conclude with "thirty-one kings in all." Amazing! The list of battles fought using the ROAR or shout of the Lion of the tribe of Judah is not limited to Joshua. There are many more examples: Isaiah 42:3 and 31:4, Jeremiah 25:30, Zephaniah 1:14 and 3:14, Zechariah 2:10 and 9:9, Ezekiel 43:2, and Job 37:3–5. The list goes on. But for now, we will look at Joshua in the battle for Jericho:

> *Now when Joshua was by Jericho, he looked up and saw a man standing in front of him. In his hand was his drawn sword. Joshua went to Him and said, "Are you for us or for our enemies?"*

> *The man replied, "Neither, for I am the commander of the army of the LORD. Now I have come."*
>
> *Then Joshua fell with his face to the ground and worshipped. Then he said, "What does my Lord wish to say to His servant?" The commander of the army of the LORD replied, "Remove your sandals from your feet, for the place where you are standing is holy." So, Joshua did this.*
>
> **Joshua 5:13–15 (NIV)**

Read Joshua Chapter 6:1–27 in your Bible. Let's begin by looking at the Lord's battle strategy in verses 1–7.

"Now Jericho was tightly secured before the children of Israel. There was no way of leaving or entering" (Joshua 6:1, NIV).

The people of Jericho knew that Israel was coming, and they were locked down tight.

"The LORD said to Joshua, 'See, I have given Jericho, its king, and mighty men of valor into your hand'" (Joshua 6:2, NIV).

The Lord is not only speaking of what Joshua could *see* with his eyes. He was also referring to the principalities and dark forces over Jericho. This is a very important principle. We cannot take the ground that the Lord has not yet delivered into our hands. He must go before us. Ezekiel

40:2–3 explains how the Lord of Hosts uses borders to mark off territory:

> *In visions of God He took me to the land of Israel and set me on a very high mountain, on whose south side were some buildings that looked like a city.*
>
> *I saw a man whose appearance was like bronze; he was standing in the gate way with a linen cord, and a measuring rod in his hand.*
>
> **Ezekiel 40:2–3 (NIV)**

The verses go on to explain how this man (who we now would say is an angel) measured off all of the boundaries around Jerusalem.

First, God measures off the boundaries He sets in place. The spiritually strong men are not supposed to go past the set boundaries for the regions that they are over. When we are taking territory for the Lord by His orders, we need to walk these same borders and boundaries, marking them off for His angel armies. Think of it as a line we are tracing for a bombing battalion to set the target in their sights.

When I was a brown belt (many years ago), I had a young instructor who was, at age fifteen, a third-degree black belt, teaching me sparing techniques one-on-one. He told me that before he ever met his opponent, he would walk the four corners of the ring, marking off his boundaries.

In following his instructions, I began to walk the ring, and it all started to make sense to me. I felt empowered. I was claiming this small territory for my victory. I marked out my boundaries in the ring and lay claim to it before the battle had even begun.

"Then The LORD said to Joshua, 'See, I have given Jericho into your hands, along with its King and fighting men. March around the city once with all the armed men. Do this for six days'" (Joshua 6:2–3, NIV).

The Lord commanded Joshua to *see* with his spiritual eyes, prophetically, into the heavenly realm so that he could understand and reflect on the fact that God had already given them victory. Joshua *sees* with his eyes of faith—God's vision of Jericho destroyed.

The words "have given" are past perfect tense. These words represent a prophetic perfection in the Hebrew text, which describes a future event or action as having already taken place.

As the Commander of the Lord's army was fighting the spiritual dark forces, He gave Joshua and the Israelites instructions to follow in a specific order. They had to wait outside the gates while the Lord of Hosts dispatched His armies from heaven in a fierce battle that was taking place over this walled city.

"For our fight is not against flesh and blood, but against principalities, against powers, against the rulers of the darkness of this world, and against spiritual forces of evil in the heavenly places" (Ephesians 6:12, NIV).

The seven priests bearing the seven rams' horn trumpets were in front of the Ark of the Lord. There were armed men in front of the Ark of the Lord. The rear guard went after the Ark while all were blowing trumpets. They marched around the city for seven days. The number seven is used eleven times in this chapter. It is important to take note of this. Seven priests, with seven trumpets, march around the city for seven days, with seven trips around the city on the seventh day.

Seven is *zayin* in the Hebrew alphabet. Read the explanation of this important number as explained by Pastor Troy Brewer, author of *Numbers That Preach*:

> *The sevenfold Spirit of God. Zayin has a complicated meaning: straight light from God to man or returning light. It also means sword of nourishment at the same time. It is used as a time divider. It is also the number of perfection.*
>
> *The number zayin is mentioned 860 times in the Hebrew Bible. If you connect the meaning of the number zayin, you could say, "The justice of the throne of God returns His light to man directly, and each ruling contains the sword of judgment against the enemy, and the nourishment of the favor of God is in the same ruling."*

> *The word zayor means to remember, and it carries in its meaning the number zayin. Also, the significance of the number seven (zayin) to the creation and the Sabbath and the fact that the Israelites were entering into their inheritance signified the beginning of the land as a prophetic picture of the Israelites coming into their time of rest with the Lord.*

"Therefore, since the promise of entering His rest still stands, let us be careful that none of you be found to have fallen short of it" (Hebrews 4:1, NIV).

The Nature of the Believers' Weapons

The spiritual weapons of our warfare are appropriated through prayer, faith, and the truth of the Word of God. Our weapons are designed to tear down the spiritual strongholds raised by Satan using spiritual forces, the world system, and our own thoughts to gain a foothold to build a fortress around where he has gained spiritual ground. This could represent personal, family, and regional strongholds. There are many spiritual weapons at our disposal. We have already spoken of the armor of God and the blood of the Lamb. Thanksgiving and praise are also weapons. There's also the "fire of God" to burn up the works of darkness and refine us into greater warriors. Holy Communion is a powerful weapon, especially for healing of the body and mind. Fasting facilitates our drawing nearer to Christ and furthering ourselves from the flesh. Calling other warrior brothers and sisters in Christ to fight alongside you is also important. Submission to the Lord is so important. (For if we submit to the Lord, then the devil must flee!) Resting in the presence of the Almighty is a key strategy. The accuser cannot reach us in the arms of the Father. Trumpets or shofar call angels to our location in the thick of battle and also call them to guard us. (Remember Ephesians 6.)

The use of trumpets was at one time on earth and is still in heavenly realms, a signal used to usher in the time of Jubilee to proclaim the presence of God during the religious feasts. Trumpets announce His presence.

Spiritual preparation is fundamental to our ability to appropriate God's strength in exchange for our weakness. Israel had been prepared to trust and obey the Lord in previous chapters, especially in Chapter 5, when He told them to consecrate themselves to Him.

In Joshua 6:8–21, Joshua instructs the Israelites not to shout a battle cry and not to let their voices be heard. Silence is a priority.

"Do not let a word come out of your mouths until the time I say to you, Shout the battle cry! Then shout!" (Joshua 6:10, NIV).

They did this for six days. On the seventh day, they circled the city seven times. The priests blew the trumpets, and at last, Joshua said to the people, "Shout the battle cry, for the LORD has given you the city!" (Joshua 6:16, NIV).

Notice that they did not shout or go in to take the city until the Lord gave them permission. We must obtain permission to go into the land we are to take for the Lord. We must wait, follow His instructions, and then when He gives us permission, we can go in after Him. That is because He has secured the spiritual atmosphere first. Waiting is an active practice.

This is the time for prayer and petition and sometimes fasting. Then silence, as we listen with our spiritual ears for the ROAR of our King Jesus.

"The LORD will fight for you while you keep silent" (Exodus 14:14, NIV).

"Be still and know that I am God" (Psalm 46:10, NIV).

We must be able to get quiet before the Lord as we rest in His presence. No complaining or distractions. Hebrews 11:30 says, "It is by faith that the walls of Jericho fell down."

The Israelites were willing to look foolish in the world's eyes as they rested in the Lord. Only He is our source of strength. Waiting is hard, and it takes endurance, but it will bring us peace in our obedience to the Lord. There are no quick solutions to taking down the strongholds of the enemy. It is only by patient, obedient endurance that we will see God move on our behalf to the glory of His name to take down the enemy.

"And He gave a loud shout like the roar of a lion. When he shouted, the voices of the seven thunders spoke" (Revelation 10:3, NIV).

As we read through Joshua Chapter 6, I can feel my heart beating faster, my courage growing, and I am filled with anticipation. All of this is welling up inside of me. I am like a crouching lion looking to pounce! Then, with one final round of the city, the Lord gives the signal, and Joshua tells the Israelites to shout! I picture it looking something like this: the anticipation bubbling over inside the army of Israel. Their confidence is growing daily. When the battle for the spiritual atmosphere comes to its climax on the seventh day, the Lord, strong and mighty, releases His ROAR! At the exact same time, every Israelite marching around that city ROARS, with the authority of heaven, in unison with the Lord!

"And I heard a sound from heaven like the roar of rushing waters and like a loud peal of thunder. The sound I heard was like that of harpists playing their harps" (Revelation 14:2, NIV).

Jesus uses His thunderous ROAR to vanquish not only the spiritual fighting men and their king; He also inhabits the ROAR of His beloved Israel! All at once, the enemy is destroyed in both realms at once! Don't you just want to shout, Hallelujah?

Joshua Chapter 6:22–27 is a picture of God's promise to His beloved Israel. God is faithful to His word. He keeps His promises.

"Every good and perfect gift is from above, coming down from the father of heavenly lights, who does not change like shifting shadows. He chose to give us birth through the word of truth, which we might be a kind of first fruits of all He created" (James 1:17–18, NIV).

God is generous to us. "The LORD is not slow in keeping His promises as some understand slowness. Instead, He is patient with us, not wanting anyone to perish, but everyone to come to repentance" (2 Peter 3:9, NIV).

He is faithful. The prophecy of verse 26 came to be fulfilled in the days of Ahab.

"In Ahab's time, Heil the Bethelite rebuilt Jericho. He laid its foundations at the cost of his firstborn son Abiram. And set up its gates at the cost of his youngest son Segub, in accordance with the word of the LORD, spoken by Joshua son of Nun" (1 Kings 16:34, NIV).

VISION:

JUNE 26, 2018, AWAKEN, ARISE!

Today, as I was praying in my heavenly language, I was kneeling with the authority of the Lord, repeating in my spirit out loud, "Awaken! Arise!" Over and over again, I repeated these words with a sense of urgency. The Lord then prompted me to stand and sing the song "Dry Bones" by Lauren Daigle as a declaration.

Earlier in the week, the Lord showed me an angel with what I can only describe as a giant dandelion in his hand. The angel was blowing on it to disperse the seeds. I asked my Lord, "What am I seeing?" The Holy Spirit said that some of the seeds will fall on stony ground. Some seeds that fall on the path will be eaten by spirit birds, and still, more seeds have fallen in the fields and will be choked out by weeds as they begin to grow. More seeds will land in well-cared-for soil that has been prepared by angels who have gone ahead of us.

We are to water the seeds through the gifts of the Spirit (miracles, signs, and wonders), which will bring about an awakening in our spirit for those who have been sleeping. "Wake up," says the Holy Spirit. "Arise and go into the harvest!"

The first thing I did after I wrote down what was revealed was to go back and read "The Parable of the Sower" in Matthew 13. I believe that the Lord is calling His bride to awaken and arise, go into the harvest. No more sleepy Christians on Sunday morning sitting in rows and then continuing on with life as if time is on our side. Time is not on the side of those who slumber.

"And do this, understanding the present time: The hour has already come for you to wake up from your slumber because our salvation is nearer now than when we first believed" (Romans 13:11, NIV).

CHAPTER 3:
THE RELUCTANT WARRIOR

Right now, I can feel some of you thinking, *Um, yeah, that's not me. I am no warrior. I'm just a [fill in the blank, for example, housewife, barista]...*

Well, I have news for you. There was a guy named Gideon who felt the same way. This is his story.

Judges 6 begins like the reading of a script for a blockbuster movie.

> *The Israelites did evil in the eyes of the LORD, and for seven years he gave them into the hands of the Midianites. Because the power of Midian was so oppressive, the Israelites prepared shelters for themselves in mountain clefts, caves and strongholds.*
>
> **Judges 6:1–2 (NIV)**

> *Whenever the Israelites planted their crops, the Midianites, Amalekites and other eastern peoples invaded the country. When the*

> *children of Israel cried out to the LORD because of Midian, the LORD sent them a prophet who said, "Thus says the LORD, God of Israel: I brought you up from Egypt and out of that place of slavery. I delivered you from the hands of Egypt and all your oppressors. I drove them out from before you and gave you their land. I said to you, 'I AM the LORD your God. Do not worship the gods of the Amorites in whose land you are living. But you have disobeyed Me.'"*
>
> **Judges 6:7–10 (MEV)**

Gideon, son of Joash, was threshing wheat in a winepress to hide it from the Midianites. The angel of the Lord appeared and said to him,

> *"The LORD is with you, O mighty man of valor." Then Gideon said to Him, "O my lord, if the LORD is with us then why has all this happened to us? Where are all His miracles that our fathers told us about? They said, 'Did not the LORD bring us out of Egypt?' Yet now the LORD has forsaken us and delivered us into the hands of the Midianites." Then the LORD turned to him and said, "Go in this strength of yours. Save Israel from the control of Midian. Have I not sent you?" And he said to Him, "O my LORD how can I save Israel? Indeed, my clan is the weakest in Manasseh, and I am the youngest in my father's house."*

> Then the LORD said to him, "But I will be with you, and you will strike the Midianites as one man."
>
> **Judges 6:12–16 (MEV)**

In verse 12, the Lord called Gideon a mighty warrior! He did not consider Gideon by his outward appearance.

He did not consider Gideon based on Gideon's own assessment of himself and his clan. The Lord called to Gideon's *spirit man* and awoke in him his true potential in God. He prophesied over Gideon, and his true potential then came forth from being dormant in the earthly realm. He became the warrior in the flesh that God knew him to be in the spirit. When God calls out to you as a "mighty warrior," you are who God says you are! Stand in the authority of who He has called you to be and walk in it!

My heart longs for women from all walks of life to understand their identity and full potential in Christ. Our worth is not in earthen vessels.

"But we have this treasure in jars of clay to show that this all-surpassing power is from God and not from us" (2 Corinthians 4:7, NIV).

Our worth is in the cross of Christ! He ransomed heaven to buy us back from death!

"For this reason, Christ is the mediator of a new covenant, that those who are called may receive the promised eternal inheritance now that He has died as a ransom to set them free, from the sins committed under the first covenant" (Hebrews 9:15, NIV).

Ransom: noun, "a sum of money or other payment demanded or paid for the release of a prisoner."

I want us to think about that for a moment. *Selah!*

> *So, Gideon went and prepared a young goat and unleavened bread from an ephah of flour. He put the meat in a basket, and he put the broth in a pot, and brought them out and offered them to Him under the oak.*
>
> *And the angel of the LORD said to him, "Take the meat and the unleavened bread, lay them on this rock. And pour out the broth."*
>
> *So, Gideon did.*
>
> *The angel of the LORD reached out His staff that was in His hand and touched the meat and unleavened bread. Fire rose out of the rock and consumed the meat and unleavened bread. Then the angel of the LORD departed from His sight.*
>
> *Then Gideon perceived that it was indeed the angel of the LORD.*
>
> *So, Gideon said, "Alas, O LORD God! I have seen the angel of the LORD face to face."*
>
> *Then the LORD said to him, "Peace be with you. Do not be afraid. You will not die."*
>
> *Then Gideon built an altar to the LORD and called it The LORD is peace. Even to this*

day, it stands in Ophrah of the Abiezrites.

Judges 6:19–24 (MEV)

Gideon made an offering to the Lord, and the Lord accepted it. It sealed the oath between them. Realizing that this was indeed the Lord of Hosts, with whom he had just had an encounter, Gideon freaked out! Oh my! *I saw God face to face!* The Lord had to calm him down with the reassurance that he would not die. I love this! Seriously, aren't we just like that when we encounter the Holy Spirit tugging on us? Many of us freak out momentarily. Our heartbeat quickens, and we begin to feel uncomfortable. We begin shifting around in our seats, or if we are out in public somewhere, we may look around us to see if anyone else felt that nudge. Perhaps some of us even talk ourselves out of believing that we have actually really had an encounter with God. We let it pass. The moment fades *if* we do not heed the call.

If we do not respond, eventually, His voice begins growing ever fainter in our spirit until, one day, our ears do not perceive Him calling to us.

I believe God is calling to us as the church to come alive! Awaken and arise! I have heard this repeated phrase in my spirit many times. I believe He is specifically calling women to the front lines. I don't want to remain in a valley of dry bones, dead to the plight of the world in its desperation! I refuse to let my potential in Christ be squandered away in wasted time! I want everything that God wants for me. I don't want to limit His work in me by ignoring His voice. God is calling to His beloved daughters, "Come alive! Awaken! Arise!" Will you accept the invitation?

> *The hand of the LORD was upon me, and He brought me out by the Spirit of the LORD and set me in the middle of a valley; it was full of bones. He led me back and forth among them, and I saw a great many bones on the floor of the valley, bones that were very dry. He asked me, "Son of man, can these bones live?"*
> I said, "Sovereign LORD, only you alone know."
>
> **Ezekiel 37:1–3 (MEV)**

In Judges Chapter 6, verses 25–26, we next find our hero fast asleep when the Lord says to him,

> *Take a bull from your father's herd and a second bull seven years old. Tear down your father's Baal altar and cut down the Asherah pole beside it.*
>
> *Then build an altar to the LORD your God on top of this stronghold in an orderly way. Take the second bull and offer it as a burnt offering with the wood of the Asherah pole that you will cut down.*
>
> **Judges 6:25–26 (MEV)**

This is one of the first steps in taking back territory from our enemies in the spirit realm. With God's permission, we go into a stronghold and dedicate the territory over that region back to the Lord. We can take back our families, our husbands and children, our homes, our neighborhoods, our cities, and our churches from the enemy.

I personally take my youngest son's guitar into my hands and pray for him while I am holding it up before the Lord. We can take back God's territory, where the devil has invaded our lives by trickery and deception, if we will only awaken in the spirit and declare our submission to the Lord for our lives and our loved ones. I want to fulfill my destiny in Christ! I want my family and loved ones to do so, too. I want us to not just survive; I want us to thrive in our circumstances.

Gideon had humbled himself and submitted his life to God's will. That is why he was able to take down the places of idol worship. He and God were in agreement. He obeyed God and did as the Lord told him to do. He didn't brush off the feeling in his gut as though it were indigestion. He awakened in his spirit man.

That is where we will find the warrior we were meant to be: at the feet of Jesus.

"Submit yourselves, then, to God. Resist the devil, and he will flee from you. Come near to God and He will come near to you. Wash your hands, you sinners, and purify your hearts, you double-minded" (James 4:7–8, MEV).

> *All the Midianites, and Amalekites and the people from the east gathered together and*

they crossed over and they camped in the valley of Jezreel.

The Spirit of the LORD enveloped Gideon. He blew a Ram's horn trumpet and the Abiezrites assembled behind him.

He sent messengers throughout all of Manasseh and they assembled behind him as well. He also sent Messengers to Asher, Zebulun, and Naphtali, so these tribes came up to meet him.

Gideon said to God, "If you will use my hands to save Israel, as You have said—I am placing a fleece of wool on the threshing floor. If there is dew on the fleece only and all of the ground remains dry, I will know that You will save Israel with my hands, as You have said."

So, it happened. He got up the next morning and squeezed the fleece. Enough dew poured out of the fleece to fill a bowl full of water.

Then Gideon said to God, "Do not let your anger burn against me as I speak only one more time. Please let me perform a test with the fleece one more time. Please let the fleece be the only thing dry, and let there be dew on all of the ground."
So, God did this during that night. Only the fleece was dry, and the dew was on all the ground.

Judges 6:33–40 (MEV)

The significance of the fleece is that it is a prophetic picture of God's sheep. The dew is a symbol of the Holy

Spirit filling us to overflowing with living water. When the fleece was full of water, and the surrounding ground was dry, this speaks of God's work in and through His people who are filled with His Spirit.

When the ground was wet, and the fleece was dry, that means God's Spirit is not resting on His people. Maybe they are dry because they are not really pursuing God. A halfway commitment to Christ will leave you dry and barren. You will feel tired and empty. Like the one Gideon had, an all-in attitude will position you for God's Spirit to rest on you, and you will run through troops and leap over enemy strongholds.

"Whoever believes in me, as Scripture has said, rivers of living water will flow from within them" (John 7:38, NIV).

"With your help, I can advance against a troop. With my God, I can scale a wall" (Psalm 18:29, NIV).

CHAPTER 4:

THE SWORD OF THE LORD AND OF GIDEON!

Are you still feeling reluctance? Chapter 7 of Judges gets more exciting! God takes Gideon's huge army down to 300 men!

The Lord said to Gideon, "You have too many people with you for me to give the Midianites into your hands, lest Israel glorify themselves over Me, saying, 'Our own power saved us'" (Judges 7:2, MEV).

The Lord told Gideon to send home anyone afraid to fight. Then, the Lord told Gideon that he still had too many men. So, the Lord sent them down to the water to drink. He tested them for Gideon there at the water's edge. The Lord told Gideon to keep those who lapped up the water by bringing their hand to their mouths and to send home the rest who knelt down to drink. That left Gideon with 300 men! Why do you think he was instructed by the Lord to keep the ones who lapped up the water with their hands? Could it be that these men showed an awareness of their surroundings that the others lacked when they leaned all the way down to the water to drink?

When your head is too low, you cannot use peripheral vision. In karate, we learn to be aware of our surroundings at all times, even going so far as to watch shadows so that no one can sneak up on us.

> *That night the LORD told Gideon, "Get up and go down into the camp, for I have given it into your hands. Yet if you are afraid to go down, then go down to the camp with Purah your servant. Listen to what they say, and afterward, you will be emboldened to go down to the camp." So he and Purah his servant went down near the camp.*
>
> *The Midianites, Amalekites and the Kedimites covered the valley like locusts, and their camels could not be counted, for they were as numerous as grains of sand on the seashore.*
>
> *Gideon came and overheard one man who was telling his dream to another. The man said, "Listen to a dream I had. I saw a dry cake of barley bread rolling into the Midianite camp. It Rolled up to a tent and struck it. It fell, turned upside down, and collapsed."*
>
> *The other man responded, "This is none other than the sword of Gideon son of Joash the Israelite. God has given Midian and the*

whole camp into his hands."

When Gideon heard the telling of the dream and its interpretation, he worshipped, returned to the camp of Israel, and said, "Get up, for the LORD has given the Midianite camp into your hands."

He divided the three hundred men into three combat units. He gave all of them the ram's horn trumpets, empty jars, and torches within the jars.

He said to them, "Look at me and do likewise. Watch, and when I come up to the perimeter of the camp and do as I do. When I and all who are with me blow the horn, then you will blow the horns all around the camp and shout, 'For the LORD and for Gideon!'"

Judges 7:9–18 (MEV)

So Gideon and a hundred men with him went to the edge of the camp at the start of the middle night watch. Then they blew the horns and smashed the jars in their hands.

The three combat units blew the horns and broke the jars. They called out, "A sword for the LORD and for Gideon!"

Every man stood in his place all around the camp, but the men in the camp ran, shouted, and fled.

> *When they blew the three hundred horns, the LORD turned every man's sword against his fellow man throughout the camp.*
>
> **Judges 7:19–22 (MEV)**

In the end, the commanders of the enemy armies and their men turned on each other and fled. The heads of the two commanders of the Midianite army were brought to Gideon on the other side of the Jordan.

There is much to be gleaned from this battle. But I am going to just hit a few key points here. Verse 9 begins with God telling Gideon, "Get up, and go down into the camp, for I have given it into your hands" (Judges 7:9, MEV).

God is not asking Gideon to go down to the camp. This is a royal command from the King to His front-line commander. Gideon quickly went from reluctance to obedience. He did what the Lord commanded him to do immediately. No hesitation. But God is kind, so out of consideration for Gideon, He told him to bring a friend. The Lord had already spoken the victory over Gideon. "For I have given it into your hands." That means it is already done. In order to further build up Gideon's confidence, He allowed Gideon to overhear how He had put fear into the hearts of the enemy army. Gideon overheard a dream that confirmed to him once again that God had already given the Midianites and their army into his hands.

God *always* confirms His word to us!

God says to Gideon, "Listen to what they say." Then the man down in the camp says to the other man he is telling his dream to, "Listen to a dream I had." (Paraphrased from the Modern English Version Spiritual Warfare Bible, Judges 7:9–22.)

Whenever God says "listen," He is actually saying so much more.

Listen: To pay attention; to hear something with thoughtful attention; give consideration. To be alert to catch an expected sound.

The other man in the camp spoke into their own defeat when he said, "This is none other than the sword of Gideon." and "God has given Midian and the whole camp into his hands."

When Gideon heard the interpretation of the dream, he did one thing immediately. He worshiped God right there at that moment. I hope I remember to give God the glory immediately when He confirms His word to me. That kind of response is from a heart totally surrendered to God.

Gideon took a cue from what the second man in the camp said. It became his battle cry! His *ROAR*! God used that man, in that moment of fear, to inspire Gideon and encourage him once more! Look at what he said on the previous page. Gideon returned to the camp emboldened. He now was commanding with authority. There was no fear in him.

"There is no fear in love. But perfect love drives out fear because fear has to do with punishment. The one who fears is not made perfect in love" (1 John 4:18, MEV).

"Those whom He predestined, He also called, and those whom He called, He also justified, and those whom He justified, He also glorified" (Romans 8:29, MEV).

Was God not for Gideon? Did He not call him? Was Gideon not justified by God confirming His promise to Him? Did the Lord not raise up a frightened farmer to become a great commander and warrior for God? Did Gideon not praise Him for the victory at God's word before he saw it in the physical realm?

What, then, shall we say in response to these things? If God is for us, who can be against us? (Romans 8:31, MEV).

There were seven watches for watchmen to guard their cities. In ancient Israel, watches were set out in three-hour shifts. We are going to look at one watch in particular through our prophetic eyes.

"I will stand my watch, and station myself at the watchtower, and I will keep watch to see what He will say to me, and what I will answer when I am reproved" (Habakkuk 2:1, MEV).

- The first watch was the transformational watch: 6 p.m. to 9 p.m.

- Then, from 9 p.m. to 12 a.m., was the night-seeking watch.
- From 12 a.m. to 3 a.m. was the transitional breakthrough watch.
- From 3 a.m. to 6 a.m. was the graveyard/ prophetic watch.
- And 6 a.m. to 9 a.m. was considered the breakthrough watch.

"Gideon and a hundred men with him went to the edge of the camp at the start of the middle night watch" (Judges 7:19, MEV).

This was the 12 a.m. to 3 a.m. watch; it was the time of transitional breakthrough. This was when the battle for the heavenly breakthrough into the earth realm began for Gideon. It was at this time that Gideon made his move! The breaking of the jars was not only a scare tactic; it was symbolic of the transitional breakthrough happening all around them. Next, they shouted their war cry! They prophetically called into the natural realm what was already accomplished in the spiritual realm by the Lord of Hosts and His heavenly armies! This is important! Words from the mouths of God's children have the power to call down heavenly help! Why else would Jesus have told us how to pray in this way?

"Our Father in heaven, hallowed be Your name, Your kingdom come, Your will be done, on earth as it is in heaven" (Matthew 6:9–10, MEV).

The Lord of Hosts answered their declaration of faith by turning every man's sword against his fellow man in the enemy camp. The Israelites didn't even have to fight them. They ran away with God's beloved Israel in hot pursuit.

I will end this chapter not in my own words but in the words of one of our most excellent theologians—Charles Spurgeon. He gives such life to this battle in his own words. So, if you will oblige me, as follows is a quote from a sermon on "The Sword of the Lord and of Gideon" (Judges 7:20) in the words of Charles Spurgeon,

> *Gideon ordered his men to do two things. Covering up a torch in an earthen pitcher, he bade them, at an appointed signal, break the pitcher and let the light shine and then sound with the trumpet, crying, "The sword of the LORD and of Gideon!" This is precisely what all Christians must do.*
>
> *First, You must shine. Break the pitcher that conceals your light! Throw aside the bushel that has been hiding your candle, and shine! Let your light shine before men. Let your good works be such that when men look upon you, they shall know that you have been with Jesus!*
>
> *Then there must be the sound, the blowing of the trumpet! There must be active exhortations for the ingathering of sinners by proclaiming Christ crucified! Take the gospel to them. Carry it to their door. Put it in their way! Do*

> *not suffer them to escape it! Blow the trumpet right against their ears!*
>
> *Remember that the true war cry for the church is Gideon's watchword.*
>
> *"The sword of the Lord and of Gideon!"*

ROAR "the sword of the Lord and of Gideon" when you are going into battle! *Selah!*

OPEN VISION:
FRIDAY, MAY 19, 2017

I was restless. It was 2:30 a.m., and I was fully awake. My eyes were shut when suddenly I began to see darkness, and out of the darkness, I began to see images from before me. I saw flowers in an outline that appeared to be like white chalk on a blackboard.

In the flowers, as they opened into full bloom, were the silhouettes of women's faces, which looked like a cameo pendant. Each flower and woman in the cameo was different. Sometimes, there were two silhouettes in one bloom. All of the flowers appeared to be different types of roses. I asked the Lord, "Father, what does this mean?"

He said, "Song of Solomon, Rose of Sharon." So, I got up and wrote down the vision and then went straight to my Bible and began to read Chapter 2:1–4 of Song of Solomon.

> *I am a rose of Sharon, a lily of the valleys.*
>
> *Like a lily among thorns is my darling among the maidens.*
>
> *Like an apple tree among the trees of the forest is my lover among the young men. I delight to sit in his shade, and his fruit is sweet to my taste. He has taken me to the banquet hall and his banner over me is love.*

> *My lover spoke to me, "Arise my darling, my beautiful one, and come with me. See the winter has passed; the rains are over and gone. The flowers appear on the earth; the season of singing has come; the cooing of doves is heard in our land.*
>
> **Song of Solomon 2:1–4, 10–12 (NIV)**

I believe He is saying that many great women of the Bible went through dark times, but when the time was right, He brought them into bloom and put them on full display in high places.

I believe the silhouettes were women from the Bible: Esther, Deborah, Ruth, Miriam, Mary, etc.

I believe the Lord is saying to His bride, His beautiful woman who bears His image and who carries His anointing, "You are being brought out of the dark forests—the darkness of confusion, suffering, persecution, sickness, and ruin—into bloom in My presence. Come with Me and sit in My protective shadow, and you will begin to bloom, and as you bloom, you will enjoy Communion with Me, for My banner over you is love! My banner says to all powers and principalities and dark forces, 'Hands off! This is My lover, and I am well-pleased with her.' I am taking you into the public eye, and My approval is set upon you. You will be in full bloom before the eyes of man and in the spirit realm, and you will openly sing and rejoice in Me in the company of people of influence, and they will listen with their ears attentive to the message of My love."

Glory to God in the highest! Hallelujah! Let the glory of the Lord be seen, and let His praises be heard as His maidens go forth in song!

CHAPTER 5:

THE SONG OF DEBORAH!

On that day Deborah and Barak the son of Abinoam sang this song:

When the leaders in Israel dedicate themselves, and the people volunteer, you should all bless ADONAI the God of Israel.

Hear, kings; listen, princes; I will sing praises to ADONAI the God of Israel.

Judges 5:1–3 (MEV)

Louder than the sound of archers at the watering-holes will they sound as they retell the righteous acts of ADONAI, the righteous acts of his rulers in Israel.

Then ADONAI's people marched down to the gates.

Awake, awake, Deborah!

Awake, awake, break into song!

> *Arise, Barak! Lead away your captives, son of Abinoam!*
>
> **Judges 5:11–12 (MEV)**

"May all your enemies perish like this, ADONAI; But may all those who love Him be like the sun, going forth in its glory!" (Judges 5:31, MEV).

I recommend pausing here and reading the entire song of Deborah. Chapter Five of Judges is solely devoted to this song. It is beautifully poetic and will exhort you in spirit! The song of Deborah could easily be called "The *ROAR* of Deborah." As she rode out into battle at the side of the king, she was singing praises to Adonai. Can't you just picture her with her sword raised, belting the praises of the Lord our God? Sometimes, a battle cry is a shout. Sometimes, a battle cry is the sound of God's children in worship. God fights for us in those times when we are worshiping Him in spite of what is happening in or around us.

When we *ROAR* His praises and remember His goodness in song, strongholds come tumbling down! When we are singing His praises and glory, we are declaring His character, His faithfulness, and His love for His children. But wait, *is it okay for a woman of God to be a warrior?* Let's look more closely at the prophetic significance of Deborah.

As I sat on the floor in my living room one day in the late 1990s, I began to pray the Psalms, and I poured out my heart to the Father.

I had been wounded by people in my church family, and I was struggling to make sure that I was not holding on to bitterness or unforgiveness.

I began to cry.

"I just don't get it, God! I am Yours. I only want to serve You. Why am I met with such great resistance? What is the purpose of all of this? Show me what Your will is for me in Your kingdom, Lord. Why did You make me a warrior if I am not allowed to be a warrior? Do You raise up women warriors?"

As I poured out my heart to Jesus, I felt His reassurance and peace.

This is the first open vision that I can remember. I saw Jesus lean down and kiss me on my head as I was crying there on my floor. My eyes were closed, but I saw Him. I stopped crying. I opened up His Word once more, and I came right to a place in the Word of God that I had never taken notice of before. I had read through it several times. It just never stood out to me until that day.

"Now Deborah, a prophet, the wife of Lappidoth, was leading Israel at that time. She held court under the Palm of Deborah, between Ramah and Bethel in the hill country of Ephraim and the Israelites went up to her to have their disputes decided" (Judges 4:4–5, NIV).

As I began to read about Deborah, my spirit leaped from within me. I realized she was not only a prophet of

God, but she led Israel. Deborah was a mighty woman of God, a wife, and a mother. People respected her because of her godly wisdom and good counsel.

Judges 4:1–3 explains how Israel had disobeyed God once again, and they had been under heavy discipline. The Lord sold them into the hands of the king of Canaan, who reigned in Hazor. He had a war commander named Sisera, who was merciless.

Sisera had heavy firepower. He had nine hundred chariots. He cruelly oppressed the Israelites for twenty years. So, once more, they cried out to the Lord for help.

Deborah's name translates as "bee," taken from the Hebrew root word *dabar*, also meaning to arrange, speak, or subdue. She was married to Lapidoth, whose name means to "shine like a lamp." She sat under the "palm tree of Deborah" as the place of judgment. She used to sit between Ramah, which means "high place," and Bethel, which means "house of God." Ephraim is translated as "fruitfulness." You could say Deborah, "a prophetess, one who speaks, arranges and subdues by the power of God, the wife of Lappidoth, the one who shines like a lamp," was judging Israel at that time. She used to sit under the palm tree of Deborah, the place of righteousness, between the high place and seat of idolatry and the house of God, on the hill country of fruitfulness, and the sons of Israel came up to her for judgment. Deborah's job was to declare God's will to His people and to keep them from going astray.

Remember, verse 2 of Chapter 4 says the Lord sold them into the hands of King Jabin (Intellect) of Canaan, who ruled in Hazor, which is translated as "fenced in, surrounded, a village, town or yard." This imagery suggests that Jabin is not just a man; he is ruled by a territorial spirit, which can also represent our intellect, and reigns over a "fenced-in village." (A spiritual stronghold set up in our mind.) We get into agreement with these spirits of intellect, and then we think we know better than God. This gives territorial spirits permission to set up strongholds, "fencing in" our understanding of the Word of God. In other words, we can't get out of our own heads and into God's heart. We need to have God's heart to understand His Word. After all, Jesus is the Word. The spoken Word becomes spirit-filled and speaks life as we declare Jesus's name over our families and territories. This is also true in the reverse.

When we think we know more than God, or we ignore His warnings, we may speak carelessly, and in so doing, we give the devil fodder to feed on. He gains ground, and we lose the ability to understand the things of the Lord that are on His heart for His kingdom and His glory. We need to put on the mind of Christ!

"For who has known the mind of the Lord, that he may instruct him? But we have the mind of Christ" (1 Corinthians 2:16, NIV).

"Do not conform to the pattern of this world, but be transformed by the renewing of your mind. Then you will be able to test and approve what God's will is—His good, pleasing and perfect will" (Romans 12:2, NIV).

> *Deborah sent for Barak. She said to Him, "The LORD, the God of Israel, commands you: 'Go take with you ten thousand men of Naphtali and Zebulun and lead them up to Mount Tabor.*
>
> *I will lead Sisera, the commander of Jabin's army, with his chariots and his troops to the Kishon River and give him into your hands.'"*
>
> *Barak said to her, "If you go with me I will go, but if you don't go with me I won't go."*
>
> *"Certainly I will go with you," said Deborah. But Because of the course you are taking, the honor will not be yours, for the LORD will deliver Sisera into the hands of a woman." So Deborah went with Barak to Kedesh.*
>
> *There Barak Summoned Zebulun and Naphtali, and ten thousand men went up under his command. Deborah also went up with him.*
>
> **Judges 4:6–10 (NIV)**

Barak's name is translated as "lightning" and "flashing sword." His father's name (Abinoam) is translated as "father of pleasantness." Barak came from Kedesh-Naphtali. Kedesh means "to consecrate," and Naphtali means "my wrestling." The flashing sword, Barak, is the son of the father of pleasantness. They dwell in a place that is consecrated—wrestling. This could be symbolic of how we wrestle with the Word of God (Jesus) in our lives. Remember that Jacob wrestled with God. Jacob walked away with a limp (Genesis 32:25, 32:31).

Wrestling with God in our minds is futile. The Lord will sooner or later bring us to submission. Either by our own exhaustion or by getting us in a "locked" position until we tap out! Have you ever been in a grappling match? I have. For every move I make, my opponent has a countermove. This is not only true with God; it is also true with Satan.

The difference here is that God wants us to submit to His will because He knows what He wants for us is in our best interests. But the devil will lure you into his clutches by enticing you through your lusts and desires and through your wounded soul through offense and fear. Past hurts can be a big place of wrestling with God and with Satan. Many of these things, lusts and desires, are in us because of our own selfishness. We want to do things our own way. We don't believe that we can be trapped in sin. But the devil is quite the grappling expert. He will lure you in, and then he will get you into a locked position and tighten his coils around you until you can't breathe or break free from his stranglehold. His ultimate goal is to get you to "tap out" so that he can rule your life until he brings you to destruction.

I like God's way better, don't you? God wants to heal our hurts and wounds all the way down to our souls. But we grapple with His call to submit to Him.

Our Father is patient, not wanting *anyone* to perish. So, as we try our best to grapple with His will for us, He keeps countering our position so that, eventually, we tap out. Once we give in to His will, we realize that it was the best for us that He had in mind, and then we wonder why we wrestled with God in the first place.

"Therefore, submit yourselves to God. Resist the devil and he will flee from you" (James 4:7, MEV).

If you are in a "locked" position and you would like to be set free, pray with me,

Father God, gracious and kind. You love me enough not to let me be comfortable in sin or denial about my past. You love me enough to accept me when I wrestle with Your will for my life. I submit my life and my own will today to Your good and perfect will for me. I repent of past hurts that I have held onto. I let them go now. I forgive those who have hurt me. I confess any sin in my life. And now, Lord, I "tap out" to You. Let Your will be done. I declare that the devil must lose my soul, and I am no longer in agreement with the strongholds that he has used to hold me in a "locked" position. I now declare my allegiance to the Lord, Jesus Christ, the Lion of the tribe of Judah! Jesus, You are my King, and I serve You. I serve Father, Son, and Holy Spirit! In the name of Jesus, let Your Spirit cast out any spirit in me that I have been in agreement with that is from the enemy camp. I surrender, Lord! Fill me up to overflowing with Your Spirit! Amen.

Now that we have been set free, we can take our stand against the devil. We can stand in agreement with God for our families. We can begin to take back our territory, which is part of our heavenly inheritance, as co-heirs with Christ.

> *"Deborah Said to Barak, GO! This is the day the LORD has given Sisera into your hands. Has not the LORD gone ahead of you?" So Barak went down Mount Tabor, with ten thousand men following him.*
>
> *At Barak's advance, the LORD routed Sisera and all his chariots and army by the sword, and Sisera got down from his chariot and fled on foot.*
>
> *Barak pursued the chariots and army as far as Harosheth Hagoyim, and all Sisera's troops fell by the sword; not a man was left.*
>
> **Judges 4:14–16 (NIV)**

Sisera fled on foot to a tent where a woman named Jael was waiting for him. She gave him milk to drink and put a blanket over him. As he slept, she put a tent peg through his head. Verse 22 ends with this, "So, He [Barak] went up with her [Jael] and there lay Sisera with the tent peg through his temple—dead" (Judges 4:22, NIV).

"On that day God subdued Jabin king of Canaan before the Israelites. And the hand of the Israelites pressed harder and harder against Jabin king of Canaan until they destroyed him" (Judges 4:23–24, NIV)

We must never give up fighting for our families! This is such a great example of how we must press in harder and harder against the spiritual fighting men. The best way to press in harder to the fight is actually to press harder into the Lord's presence. He is a strong tower. We stand firm in Him, and He does the fighting for us. "Then you will be able to take a stand during these evil days. And after you have done everything you can, you will still be standing" (Ephesians 6:13, NIV).

This is what victory looks like from the winning side! Is it okay for a woman to be a warrior? You better believe it is! Here is a prophetic word that the Spirit of the Lord shared with me in my quiet time with Him in May 2017:

A CLARION CALL TO MOTHERS

To Travail: Painfully difficult, burdensome work; toil, pain, anguish, or suffering resulting from mental or physical hardship.

The following Scripture references prove the prophecy: Genesis 3:20; Judges 5:7–15; Luke 15:3–5, 20–24.

To the mothers of all of the living: arise!

Those who are mothers of tribes, tongues, and nations, wake up! Wake up! Break out in song…

You are called to love them, to woo them in the name of the Lord. Go down into the valley where there is much searching of heart. Pray for the prodigals. Mothers are in mourning as their young have been lied to and led off into slavery.

Join in their mourning song! Travail for the individual. "Go and get them and bring them back, O Lord!" said the mothers of the lost who are still living.

"Cry out! Cry out! And I will hear your offerings," says the Lord; your offerings are given in travail for the prodigal, the lost, and the orphan.

Cry out for the individuals and for the nations! I will bring them home to My heart because I have heard your travailing; your tears are an acceptable offering before My throne.

Each tear is precious before the Ancient of Days! Join together, united in one purpose. Ask Me to move, and I will move heaven and earth to bring back your children.

I know what it is to love as a mother loves her child. I Am the Author and Finisher of love, unconditional! See what I will do as your sons and daughters begin to come to their senses.

I have good plans for them. Even now, I am rejoicing that it is done already in heaven!

Cry out in one voice, and I will align heaven and earth to bring each one back! Look! Here they come... With much rejoicing, they come as I receive them into My open arms.

Your arms are My arms. Your hearts are My heart. Your children were My children first! It is My will that none should perish but that all would be saved.

So, cry out to Me, and I will bring them home. Home to nations, home to families, home to My heart!

"You keep track of all my sorrows. You have collected all of my tears in a bottle. You have recorded each one of them in your book" (Psalm 56:8, NIV).

Let's pray and ask God to show us our true identity in Him.

Father, we humble our hearts before You and bring our minds to attention in Your mighty presence. Father, we are all in agreement under the cross of Christ that You would bring heaven to earth and touch us by Your Spirit. Lord, we ask You to show us our true identity in Christ Jesus. And also make our assignment in You sure. Confirm it to our hearts. We know that in You, we can do all that You ask of us. Apart from You, we can do no good thing. Jesus, Lord, give us Your heart and love for people. And enable us to walk in Your authority so that we can bring Your freedom to our families and friends and churches and neighborhoods. You told us in Matthew 10:8 that You want us to heal the sick, raise the dead, cleanse those who have leprosy, and drive out demons. Freely, You have given. Freely, we receive the gifts of the Spirit. And freely, we will also give!

In Jesus Christ of Nazareth's holy name, and in the name of the Lion of the tribe of Judah, and the Lamb who was slain, we pray, amen!

CHAPTER 6:

GIANT SLAYERS

What makes a giant slayer?

The heart of the lamb that was slain and the authority of the Lion of the tribe of Judah is what makes a giant slayer.

> *Then one of the elders said to me, "Do not weep! See, the Lion of the Tribe of Judah, the root of David, has triumphed. He is able to open the scroll and its seven seals."*
> Then I saw a Lamb, looking as if it had been slain, standing at the center of the throne, encircled by the four living creatures and the elders.
>
> **Revelation 5:5–6 (NIV)**

The authority of the Lion of the tribe of Judah is the authority of Christ. All things have been given to Him and have been put under His feet. When we understand our identity in Christ Jesus, we are able to walk in His authority. We put on Christ, and we have His strength and authority to accomplish His will. He is our identity.

> *For through the law, I died to the law so that I might live for God; I have been crucified with Christ, and I no longer live, but Christ lives in me. The life I now live in the body, I live by faith in the son of God, who loved me and gave himself for me.*
>
> **Galatians 2:19–20 (NIV)**

"For in Him we live and move and have our being. As some of your poets have said, we are His offspring'" (Acts 17:28, NIV).

Read Colossians 3:12–17 in your Bible. We are to put on Christ… This is what is meant by the authority of the Lion of the tribe of Judah and of the Lamb who was slain.

This is also the beginning of understanding the heart of Christ for His beloved. The Lion is the authority of Christ; the Lamb is the heart of Christ.

We must fight from a place of resting in His presence. That is how we stay in our identity in Him. We should never move out of God's protection over us. We must have His heart for people and see through His eyes. We must love from His heart.

Sometimes, the Lord will want us to lean forward in battle; that is where His authority comes in. Sometimes, we have to lean back into Him. That is when His heart comes in. We must stay under His wings of protection and listen and obey and stay submitted, and we will be ready for what ground He calls us to fight for.

Why don't you pray with me to ask God to show you your true identity in Him?

Father, we humble our hearts before You and bring our minds to attention in Your mighty presence. Father, we are all in agreement, under the cross of Christ, that You would bring heaven to earth and touch us by Your Spirit. Lord, we ask You to show us our true identity in Christ Jesus. And also make our assignment in You sure. Confirm it to our hearts. We know that in You, we can do all that You ask of us. Apart from You, we can do no good thing. Jesus, Lord, give us Your heart and love for people. And enable us to walk in Your authority so that we can bring Your freedom to our families and friends and churches and neighborhoods. You told us in Matthew 10:8 that You want us to heal the sick, raise the dead, cleanse those who have leprosy, and drive out demons. Freely, You have given. Freely, we receive the gifts of the Spirit. And freely, we will also give!

In Jesus Christ of Nazareth's holy name, and in the name of the Lion of the tribe of Judah and the Lamb who was slain, we pray, amen!

I can think of no one better than David, whom the Lord Himself called "a man after My own heart." When it comes to giant slayers, David is our model.

"And when he had removed him, he raised up unto him David to be their king; to whom also he gave their testimony, and said, I have found David the son of Jesse, a man after mine own heart, which shall fulfill all my will" (Acts 13:22, NIV).

Our story begins in 1 Samuel Chapter 17 on two hills opposite each other with a valley in between. With the Hebrews dominating the hill country of Judea and the Philistines controlling the coastal plain, the buffer between these armies was the Shephelah. The word "Shephelah" means "low lands," but in its root, there are two Hebrew words that are used to describe God.

The valleys of the Shephelah separated the hill country and the coastal area, specifically, the Philistines and the international highway. Judah's control of the Shephelah served as a measurement of Israel's strength. Five valleys cut in an east-west direction through Shephelah and offered convenient passages from the Philistine Plain to the hill country of Judea. The valley of Elah was one of them.

"A champion named Goliath, who was from Gath, came out of the Philistine camp. His height was 6 cubits and a span" (1 Samuel 17:4, NIV).

The word "champion" here is used in the Hebrew form, meaning middle man or the man between two. This was a man who stood between these two armies and fought for his army. As Goliath comes forward with all of his armor on and his shield-bearer is holding his shield up in front of Goliath, Goliath taunts Israel's army.

> *Goliath stood and shouted to the ranks of Israel, "Why do you come out and line up for battle? Am I not a Philistine, and are you not the servants of Saul? Choose a man and have him come down to me.*
>
> *If he is able to come down and kill me, we will become your subjects; but if I do overcome him and kill him, you will become our subjects and serve us."*
>
> *Then the Philistine said. "This day I defy the armies of Israel! Give me a man and let us fight each other."*
>
> *On hearing this, Saul and all the Israelites were dismayed and terrified.*
>
> **1 Samuel 17:8–11 (NIV)**

This is one of Satan's favorite tactics: fear! The battle is lost before the Israelites even fight the Philistines because the Israelites have already become afraid. As the Spirit of the Lord had left Saul in 1 Samuel 16:14, so went Saul's courage. The Bible says three hundred and sixty-five times, "Do not be afraid." Why do you think that is? The answer is that the battle is not ours to fight. The battle always belongs to God. So, we should pick our fights carefully. Before we get all passionate about some cause or other, we should check our motives with God.

If we run into a fight of our choosing and not of God's choosing, we will most likely walk away wounded, if we walk away at all. Now, when I say check our motives, I mean, why do you feel you need to fight? Is it because of hurt or offense? Is it from fear? Or are your motives true to who you are in Christ? We as believers should be quick to listen, slow to speak, and slow to anger, for man's wrath does not produce the righteousness of God (James 1:19–20).

We need to make sure we are in the right standing with Christ and in agreement with His plan. We must be sure that we have the heart of our Lord.

A PROPHETIC DREAM I HAD IN JULY 2017

I was with a lot of people in what seemed to be an airplane hangar. We were being held there. I heard a loud noise from outside of the hangar that was coming closer and closer. It sounded like an aircraft. As I made my way to the front of the crowd, I saw standing before the double doors of the hangar a giant man. He was intentionally blocking the doors and trying to keep us all inside and didn't want us to look outside.

I could see a little bit of daylight past him. I was straining, trying to see outside to find out what the noise was. I heard myself say, "It's coming this way."

I tried to see past the giant, and he tried to distract me and keep me from getting past him. But I was able to get around him into the open.

When I looked up, I saw a blimp. It was moving past me, and it kept going. I then saw a group of fighters ready to attack. They reminded me of ninjas. The blimp had lowered them down to where I was at.

I looked around me and realized that I was not alone. Many of the teammates that I used to compete with when I was in karate tournaments were with me. And so was our master instructor.

We all suited up for battle together and began to fight off the attackers. As I looked around and realized the last fighter for the opposition had been defeated by us, all of the black belts, including me, bowed and took a knee in respect for our master instructor.

My instructor called to me to stand with him as the others stayed on their knee. In front of everyone, he gave me a gold coin, a challenge coin, a small medallion bearing an organization's insignia or emblem and carried by the organization's members. The coin had an inscription that I could not read. It was in a heavenly language. All of them bowed to me as a sign of respect.

Now, before you think I am having delusions of grandeur, let me explain that in the martial arts community, we bow to each other like you would shake a hand in respect. It doesn't make you higher than anyone else or lower to bow to your teammates and instructors. It simply is a form of recognition of respect.

The large holding room with all of the people is symbolic of being held captive by the enemy.

The giant blocking the door is symbolic of the giants we face in life that keep us from moving forward. Giants like fear, wounds, battle fatigue, and so on.

The blimp is symbolic of a promotion; it dropped off the fighters, but we won the battle.

The black belts are symbolic of the saints I battle together with against the enemy in the spirit realm.

The master instructor represents a person of authority: God.

We overcame our attackers and the giants in the land. We got through the door that the giant was blocking and fought off our enemies in the "New Land." Because of our courage and victory, God honored me with a promotion and a treasure.

CHAPTER 7:
DO NOT BE AFRAID, THE LORD WILL FIGHT FOR YOU

"The Lord will fight for you; you need only to be still" (Exodus 14:14, NIV).

David walks on the scene, the son of Jesse, the youngest of eight brothers. David has three brothers following King Saul, and they are on the front line of the battle.

The firstborn was Eliab, the second was Abinadab, and the third was Shammah. Now, in Psalm 89:27, God calls David "God's firstborn," showing us that firstborn is as much a title as a description of birth order. This example is also found in Colossians 1:15; Paul calls Jesus "Firstborn over all creation."

Paul is pointing out the preeminence of Jesus. But David was a man. He was not Jesus Himself. Why did God call him "God's firstborn?"

This is a beautiful example of knowing our identity. We, too, are "God's firstborn," having been born again by the Spirit and of water. The authority of Christ is ours also.

That is why in Matthew 18:18 (AMP), Jesus said, "I tell you the truth, whatever you forbid (bind) on earth will be forbidden in heaven, and whatever you permit (let Loose) on earth will be permitted in heaven."

Jesus is speaking of spiritual warfare, and He is speaking directly to our part in it.

He is saying that we are positional to "Him who is at the right hand of the Father," and we declare and decree God's will on earth through prayer and petition, and God, through His power, brings heaven to earth to accomplish His perfect will. It is so important that we understand this principle. It is our job as God's firstborn of the Spirit to stand in the gap for the people of the earth and even for the earth itself. As we agree with the Father in the name of Jesus, we exert our authority in Christ, and in so doing, we enforce Christ's authority on earth.

"For forty days the Philistine came forward every morning and evening and took his stand" (1 Samuel 17:16, NIV).

One day, as David was tending the sheep, his father, Jesse, asked him to go to the front lines where his three oldest brothers were and bring them an ephah of roasted grain and ten loaves of bread. "And hurry to their camp," said Jesse. "Take along these ten cheeses to the commander of their unit. See how your brothers are and bring back some assurance from them." So early in the morning, David left the flock in the care of a shepherd, loaded up, and set out as Jesse had directed.

> *Early in the morning, David left the flock in the care of a shepherd, loaded up and set out, as Jesse had directed. He reached the camp as the army was going out to its battle positions, shouting the war cry.*
>
> *Israel and the Philistines were drawing up their lines facing each other.*
>
> *David left his things with the keeper of the supplies, and ran to the battle lines and asked his brothers how they were.*
>
> *As he was talking with them, Goliath the Philistine champion from Gath, stepped out from his lines and shouted his usual defiance, and David heard it.*
>
> *Whenever the Israelites saw the man, they all fled from him in great fear.*
>
> **1 Samuel 17:20–24 (NIV)**

> *David asked the men standing near him, "What will be done for the man who kills this Philistine and removes this disgrace from Israel? Who is this uncircumcised Philistine that should defy the armies of the living God?"*
>
> **1 Samuel 17:26 (NIV)**

They told David that King Saul had promised great wealth and that the king would also give him his daughter in marriage and exempt his family from taxes in Israel. But when David's oldest brother, Eliab, heard him speaking with the men, he burned with anger at David. Eliab asked David, "Why have you come down here? And with whom did you leave those few sheep in the wilderness? I know how conceited you are and how wicked your heart is; you came down only to watch the battle" (paraphrased from the New International Version, 1 Samuel 17:28).

David's brother mistook David's comment as insolence and pride. Sometimes, that happens to us when we are full of passion for the Lord. People can mistake our passionate love affair with Christ for pride or even hubris. Don't let that squash your spirit. God will use your passion for Him when the time and season are right to do so.

"Now, what have I done?" said David. "Can't I even speak?" (1 Samuel 17:29, NIV).

David was hurt by his oldest brother's jab. David's motive was righteous. Look at what he said to the men in verse 26, "Who is this uncircumcised Philistine that he should defy the armies of the living God?" (2 Samuel 17:26, NIV).

David set his heart on the reputation of God and of Israel. Notice he says, "Armies of the living God," plural. David knows that this battle is not won in the flesh but is decided already in heaven. Heavenly armies are fighting over the region to claim it in the name of the God of Israel. David saw the battle in spiritual terms. He had a very close relationship with the Lord. He was with God alone in the wilderness as he tended sheep in the fields.

He pressed into the presence of God in those times so that when he needed to lean forward in battle (as the lion), he was already prepared. He had been leaning into God's heart out in the wilderness.

When Goliath made his arrogant statement, David burned with righteous anger. Yes, it is right to be angry when the devil comes against us. So long as we know that we are in right standing with the Lord, we can then go to God in prayer with zeal as God fights for our families, churches, neighborhoods, and righteous causes close to God's heart and so on.

We must remember that we are angry with Satan and not with God or people. God is always on the side of truth and godly justice.

> *What David said was overheard and reported to Saul, and Saul sent for him. David said to Saul, "Let no one lose heart on account of this Philistine; your servant will go and fight him."*
>
> *Saul Replied, "You are not able to go out against this Philistine and fight him; you are only a young man, and he has been a warrior from his youth."*

But David said to Saul, "Your servant has been keeping his father's sheep. When a lion or a bear came and carried off sheep from the flock, I went after it, struck it and rescued the sheep from its mouth. When it turned on me, I seized it by its hair, struck it and killed it.

Your servant has killed both the lion and the bear; this uncircumcised Philistine will be like one of them because he has defied the armies of the living God. The Lord who rescued me from the paw of the lion and the paw of the bear will rescue me from the hand of this Philistine."

Saul said to David, "Go, and the Lord be with you."

1 Samuel 17:31–37 (NIV)

The Lord will always prepare us for bigger battles by giving us lesser battles to fight. I like this verse from 1 Peter 4:12–13 (NIV), "Dear friends do not be surprised at the fiery ordeal that has come on you to test you as though something strange were happening to you. But rejoice in as much as you participate in the sufferings of Christ, so that you may be overjoyed when his glory is revealed."

Small battles lead to good training and small victories. They build our confidence in the Lord. We learn to trust Him in the little day-to-day things. Bigger battles put our trust in the Lord on display. People watch how we handle it. The Lord fights for us. It is a testimony to those who are watching us as believers. One way or another, God will have the victory. That should always be our motivation when we go to war. God will then use our faithfulness and trust in Him to manifest greater victories for His kingdom and for His namesake.

"Yet, He saved them for His name's sake, to make His mighty power known" (Psalm 106:8, NIV).

Saul dressed David up in his armor. But David was uncomfortable when he tried to walk around. So, David took it off. This is important to note.

We are not made to wear anyone else's armor but the armor of God, which is fitted to us for each battle we encounter.

How do you know if you are trying to walk around in someone else's armor? Does it fit who you are? Are you comfortable with it? Again, this is an identity issue.

We have to know who we are in Christ, put on Christ, and stop trying to fit into molds that were not crafted for us. We are all unique, and each of us has a unique purpose in His kingdom.

"Seek His kingdom first, and His righteousness and all these things will be added to you" (Matthew 6:33, ESV).

David wore the armor of God! He took the helmet of salvation, the breastplate of righteousness, and the sword of the Spirit, which is the Word of God (Ephesians 6:17). Other than that, all he had was his staff, five smooth stones in a bag, and a slingshot.

"Then he took his staff in his hand, chose five smooth stones from the stream, put them in the pouch of His shepherds' bag and, with his sling in his hand, approached the Philistine" (1 Samuel 17:40, NIV).

The staff David carried is symbolic of Christ, our Good Shepherd. Christ was born of David's bloodline.

The five smooth stones were no ordinary flat skipping stones that you would pick up from the river. They were larger, rounder, and heavier. Some ask, "Why five smooth stones?" I have heard different reasons from different studies. However, I always lean toward the prophetic signs. The number five in Hebrew represents grace. David was covered in God's grace, and grace brings protection. Grace is also favor, and God's favor rested on David as the Spirit of the Lord was upon him. Grace is the power of God, not only for saving but for sustaining. Grace is God's bearing of Himself toward His children, always in the context of loving favor.

"Cast your burden on the LORD, and He shall sustain you; He shall never permit the righteous to be moved" (Psalm 55:22, NKJV).

"For it is by grace you have been saved through faith; and that not of yourselves, it is the gift of God" (Ephesians 2:8, NKJV).

Also, Goliath came from a region that was broken up into five provinces. Goliath was one of five brothers. This shows me that God was speaking prophetically through David that not only would Goliath be defeated with one stone, but David and Israel carried the favor of God to take back all five provinces from the Philistines and destroy Goliath's lineage.

Grace is the gift that keeps on giving.

"And the Philistine cursed David by his gods" (1 Samuel 17:41, NIV).

This is what sealed Goliath's fate. Just like the devil, whom he served by worshiping his "little g" gods, Goliath overplayed his hand. There is a strategy to be gleaned here. Satan always gets overconfident and shows his hand because of his boastful nature. He can't resist! When he does this, he always ends up revealing to us his own weakness: *pride!*

Our best defense is to lean into God and worship Him. Let the Father direct us when He is ready for us to take down the giants in His name and for His glory; never for us, always for the Lord, strong and mighty!

This battle comes down to Goliath and his armor-bearer against David and the Lord of angel armies, the God of Israel! This battle was over before it began. All because young David, who was not even king yet, had the courage to fight in the name of the Lord against a foe that seemed so much bigger than he was. But who is bigger than God?

> *David said to the Philistine, "You come against me with sword and spear and javelin,*

> *but I come against you in the name of the LORD Almighty, the God of the armies of Israel, whom you have defied.*
>
> *This day the LORD will deliver you into my hands, and I'll strike you down and cut off your head. This very day I will give the carcasses of the Philistine army to the birds and the wild animals, and the whole world will know that there is a God in Israel.*
>
> *All those gathered here will know that it is not by sword or spear that the LORD saves; for the battle is the LORD'S, and He will give all of you into our hands."*
>
> **1 Samuel 17:45–47 (NIV)**

David's reply to the Philistine, "*I come in the name of the LORD, Almighty, the God of the armies of Israel,*" is a declaration to Goliath and everyone else on that battlefield. David is saying that he is God's representative and that he is on a mission from the God of angel armies. We must be like David. His motive came straight from God's heart!

How do we choose to respond when we are being attacked?

Remember how, in an earlier chapter, I mentioned being wounded by people I had trusted and loved in my church family? How I chose to respond made all the difference between me choosing to stay wounded and let those hurt feelings turn into bitter roots or being on the side of God's victory by confessing my hurt and brokenheartedness to the Father. I asked Him to remove it from me as far as the east is from the west. Just the same way we ask the Lord to remove sin in our lives. I chose to stand alone, and I did not gossip. I went straight to the source of all hope: Jesus. I poured out my heart to Him and rendered it until there were no bad feelings or negative thoughts about these people left in me. Jesus sustained me through the battle as I was finally able to ask Him to bring blessings to those who had wounded me. Now that's amazing grace!

"As the Philistine moved closer to attack him, David ran quickly toward the battleline to meet him" (paraphrased from the New International Version, Hebrews 12:15).

Bitter roots grow deep into the soil of our hearts and can even reach into our spirit man. If we don't put off strife and bitterness, we are poisoning ourselves, and in so doing, we may poison everyone else we come in contact with.

This is just what the enemy would love to see happen to God's people. He wants us to do his evil work for him by poisoning our own understanding of God's love and grace for us and then turning us loose on other believers, seeking to squash them out of a root of bitterness. The only cure for this kind of foul spirit is confession! As many times as it takes until the bitter root dies or has been uprooted by the Holy Spirit, who is working in us to make our salvation complete until the day of the Lord. Let's pause here and pray.

Dear Father, in Jesus's mighty name, I come before Your mercy seat.

I declare the blood of Jesus as our covering. I confess my broken heart and bitterness toward those who have hurt me. Whether they meant to harm me or not, I have been wounded. I do not wish to hold onto this hurt, so I leave it before the mercy seat of Christ.

Please make in me a clean heart, mind, soul, and spirit. If there is any bitter root, I ask the Holy Spirit to uproot it and burn it in the refining fire of the Lord. I forgive those who hurt me. I make a fresh start now and ask You to bless those who persecute me and make me stronger in the process.

Thank You, Lord, for Your amazing love and forgiveness for my hurts and sins. I ask You to now forgive those who have hurt me the same way You have forgiven me.

In Jesus's holy name, by His blood and by the cross, I claim the resurrection power in me now! Amen.

"The Philistine moved closer to attack him. David ran quickly toward the battle line to reach him" (1 Samuel 17:48–50, NIV).

Reaching into his bag and taking out a stone, he slung it and struck the Philistine on the forehead. The stone sank into his forehead, and he fell face down on the ground. So, David triumphed over the Philistine with a sling and a stone; without a sword in his hand, he struck down the Philistine and killed him.

But David had a part to complete in it.

First Samuel 5:4 is a prophetic look at what was to come in this battle. Goliath's "little g" god, Dagon, had fallen on his face before the Lord. Now, Goliath had fallen on his face before the Lord.

"So, David triumphed over the Philistine, with a sling and a stone. Without a sword in his hand, he struck down the Philistine and killed him" (1 Samuel 17:50, NIV).

This was to be Goliath's fate also.

David grabbed Goliath's sword and used it to behead the giant in front of God and everybody! This act served to rally the Israelite troupes, and they rose up to chase the Philistines as the Philistines tried to hightail it out of there. The Israelites went on to chase the Philistines out of their land and plundered their tents! David took the head of Goliath to Jerusalem.

"They have prepared a net for my steps; my soul is bowed down; they have dug a pit before me; into the midst of it they themselves have fallen" (Psalm 57:6, NKJV).

The devil always overplays his hand. God uses the devil's own schemes to trap him.

Here Comes Another "LOTR, The Return of the King," Reference:

On the battlefield are King Théoden and his army, known as the Rohirrim. Among them is our hero, Eowyn. She is King Théoden's niece. She has disguised herself as a soldier and rides into battle with the hobbit Merry. King Théoden is struck down to the ground by the fell beast—the witch king's dragon creature. Théoden lies on the ground as the fell beast approaches to eat him. Eowyn jumps in front of her uncle to try to save him as Merry (the humble hobbit) watches closely. The witch king is astride the fell beast and is disgusted with the soldier for jumping in front of him. Eowyn says to the witch king, "I will kill you if you touch him." He replies, "Do not come between the Nazgul and his prey."

The king looks up from the ground as the beast thrusts his head forward toward Eowyn to eat her; she bravely chops his head off with two blows from her sword. She now stands face-to-face with the witch king. He carries a mace in his hand; she has her shield up and her helmet on with her sword in her hand. She ducks, bobs, and weaves as he swings wildly at her. He makes contact with her shield, and it shatters! He grabs her by her throat! She gasps and looks at him in horror. It looks like she is going to die, and all is lost! With his hand clasped tightly around her throat, the witch king says, "No man can kill me. Die now." Merry, the humble hobbit, sees his chance and plunges the dagger he is carrying into the back of the witch king's knee, breaking the spell of immortality. The witch king falls to his knees before Eowyn. Up until now, no one except for Merry knows that she is a woman. Then, Eowyn sees her opportunity. She remembers what the prophecy over the witch king is, "No man can kill me." She heard it from his own lips! Eowyn takes off her helmet, showing herself to be a woman, and she says, "I am no man!" and she plunges the sword into what would be the witch king's face! He is vanquished!

Did you catch it? The devil always overplays his hand. He gave it away. He told her the secret to his own demise. She and Merry fulfilled their destiny that day by dispatching the witch king of Angmar.

Are you a giant slayer? You just might be. But if you don't take the risk, you will never live to your full potential in Christ.

Don't let anyone convince you that you are not meant for greater things. David did not know that God would call him to be king of Israel or part of the lineage of the line of Christ. Gideon didn't know that he could fight as a warrior until God called him to do so. Joshua carried on the work that God had begun in Moses. Deborah was a wife and a mother, as well as an ambassador, judge, and prophet.

How would you like to be remembered? All of the characters in the Bible seem larger than life. The truth is that they were just like me and you. They were ordinary, God-fearing people. They were called into service by the most high God. The difference between us and them is this: They accepted the call on their lives, and they allowed themselves to become who God called them to be.

Will You Answer the Call?

[Your name here], loving mother and a wonderful wife. She lived each day to serve Christ in her waking hours, and even at rest, her sleep was dedicated to His purpose. She was a giant slayer and had also defeated sea monsters and dragons. She was renowned for her wisdom, and people intentionally would seek her out for her sound, godly advice, but the thing that was most important to her was that she wanted to defeat evil and love as Jesus loves. She lived her life wholly devoted to Christ and His divine purposes.

Could this woman be you? You will never know if you do not step out into the deep waters and let God lift you up into heavenly places with Him. Oh, what an adventure awaits those who are willing!

CHAPTER 8:

THERE ARE NO COINCIDENCES

Esther is one of my favorite books in the Word of God. What a marvelous example of courage and trust in the Lord is on display here. While God's people were in exile under the rule of King Xerxes, they faced the possibility of annihilation.

King Xerxes had a vain wife. She was lovely, and she knew it; she was also rebellious. One night, when Xerxes was merry with wine, he sent for her. He wanted to show her beauty to the people and the officials because Vashti was very beautiful. However, the queen refused to come at the king's command. Therefore, the king grew very angry, and wrath burned within him.

The king consulted with his closest confidants, who held the highest rank in the kingdom, "According to the law, what should be done about Vashti?" One of Xerxes's men answered, "Queen Vashti has wronged not only the king but also all the princes and people who are in all the provinces of King Xerxes. For should this matter of the queen spread to all wives, then they would look with contempt on their husbands when it is reported that she never came when you ordered her to."

Memukan, the king's advisor, went on,

> *If it pleases the king, let a royal decree be sent by him, and let it be written in the laws of the whole kingdom that it may never be altered, and Vashti can never enter into the presence of King Xerxes again and the king will give her royal position to another woman who is better than she.*
>
> **Esther 1:19 (NIV)**

The king liked this and made it happen. Here is where Esther and Mordecai come into the picture.

> *Now in the citadel of Susa, there was a certain Jew named Mordecai, the son of Jair, the son of Shimei, the son of Kish, a Benjamite.*
>
> *He had been taken away from Jerusalem among the exiles and carried into captivity along with King Jeconiah of Judah by King Nebuchadnezzar of Babylon.*
>
> *He was the guardian of Hadassah, that is Esther (who was his uncle's daughter) because she had neither father nor mother.*

The young woman was lovely to look at and beautiful in form. When her father and mother died, Mordecai took her as his own daughter.

[Mordecai and Esther's lineage is important. Their bloodline is related to Jacob. Hadassah (Esther's Hebrew name) means compassion.]

Esther 2:5–7 (MEV)

Read Esther 2:8–11 in your Bible.

The turn came for each young woman to go to King Xerxes. When the young woman went to the king, she was given whatever she desired to take with her from the harem to take to the king's palace. In the evening, she went in. In the morning, she returned to the harem and would not go in to see the king again unless he delighted in her and sent for her by name. When it came time for Esther to go to the king, she took nothing with her but what the king's eunuch, Hegai, advised.

Now Esther obtained favor in the sight of all who saw her. So Esther was taken to King Xerxes at his royal house in the month of Tebeth which is the tenth month, in the seventh year of his reign.

The king loved Esther more than any other woman because she had gained grace and favor in his sight more than all the virgins. So, he set the royal crown on her head and made her queen instead of Vashti.

Esther 2:16–17 (NKJV)

Esther is made the queen, and the king throws a royal feast for her among all of his officials and servants.

> *[There was a second gathering of the virgins, and Mordecai was sitting at the King's gate.]*
>
> *Esther had not yet disclosed her lineage of her people since Mordecai had so commanded her.*
>
> *Esther followed the command of Mordecai just as she had when under his protection.*
>
> *During those days when Mordecai was sitting at the King's gate, two of the king's eunuchs, Bigthan and Teresh, who served as keepers of the door, became angry and sought to attack King Xerxes.*
>
> *But the matter became known to Mordecai, and he reported it to Queen Esther, and Esther reported it to the king in the name of Mordecai.*
>
> *When the matter was investigated and confirmed, both of the men were hanged on the gallows, and it was written in the book of the chronicles in the presence of the king.*
>
> **Esther 2:19–23 (NIV)**

In this part of the Scriptures, we can see that Mordecai's name is established before the king. This is how God positioned Mordecai and Esther in the right place at the right time. There are no coincidences in the Hebrew language. The Hebrew people believed in divine providence. God is sovereign and omnipresent. He is the author of space and time. He can and *does* orchestrate situations to place people where He wants them.

"From one man He made all the nations, that they should inhabit the whole earth; and He marked out their appointed times in history and the boundaries of their lands" (Acts 17:26, NIV).

In Chapter 2:19–23, we see that Mordecai was at the "king's gate." This is a prophetic picture. There are spiritual gateways to cities, regions, and even entire countries.

The spiritual powers over these places entered into these atmospheres from the gates. Think about it. When we enter the United States of America, what is the first thing that you think of? Is it the Statue of Liberty? That is because the statue represents a gateway to our country. Now consider this: wherever there have been idols or altars set up, these are gateways. If you look at the history of any region on earth, you will find out what spiritual powers had or have authority over which regions by the altars or idols that were and sometimes still are worshiped there.

Mordecai went to the king's gate because that is where commerce, taxes, and judgments came down from. The rulers, or those who serve them, would gather at the city gates to carry out whatever needed to be dealt with in regards to the people that were subject to them; Mordecai understood this. He was at the gate because he was a man of influence for the Jews. He was positioned there by God in opposition to Haman. (Remember Jacob and Esau in Genesis 25:19–34.)

> *After these things, King Xerxes praised Haman the son of Hammedatha the Agagite, and promoted him and set his seat above all the officials who were with him.*
>
> *[Haman's lineage is important. He is related to Esau.]*
>
> *All the king's servants, when at the gate bowed or paid homage to Haman since the king had commanded it. Mordecai, however, never bowed or paid homage.*
>
> *[Remember how earlier I explained that Mordecai is related to Jacob.]*
>
> *So the king's servants tending the king's gate said to Mordecai, "Why are you transgressing the king's commandment?"*
>
> *Though they spoke to him daily, he never listened to them, so they reported it to Haman to see if the words of Mordecai would stand, for Mordecai had told them that he was a Jew.*
>
> *When Haman saw that Mordecai neither bowed nor paid him homage, he was filled with rage.*
>
> *But he disdained to lay hand on only Mordecai since they had told him of the people of Mordecai. So Haman sought to destroy all*

the Jews throughout the whole kingdom of Xerxes.

Esther 3:1–6 (MEV)

We can see here why Mordecai refused to bow to Haman. Mordecai and Haman's lineage shows that Agagites and Jews were sworn enemies; this is found in Genesis 14:7, 36:12. Agagites came from Amelec, which is an anti-Christ spirit. They wanted to destroy God's people.

The war is between Jacob's grandson and Esau's grandson. By virtue of the fact that we are grafted into the family tree of Christ as believers and followers, it means that we are included in Jacob's bloodline. In Exodus 17:14 (NIV), the Lord says, "I will utterly blot out the name of Amelec from heaven."

Amelec believed in luck. But as I pointed out earlier, there is no such thing as luck. We believe that everything is ordained by God. God is providential. This is important. This war wages on today through spiritual powers and principalities that occupy these lands.

Both political and religious spirits will subject people to slavery in one form or another. Women and children are especially vulnerable to these powers that usually work through the hierarchy of the political and religious beliefs in these territories.

Read Esther 3:8–15 in your Bible.

Then Haman said to king Xerxes, "There exist a scattered people dispersed among the other peoples in all the provinces of your kingdom. Their laws are different from all others, and they are not complying with the king's laws, so there may not be a suitable reason for the king to allow them to exist.

If it pleases the king, may it be written that they are to be destroyed, and may there be ten thousand talents of silver deposited into the king's treasuries so that I may distribute it to the hands of those doing the work."

Esther 3:8–15 (MEV)

Did you notice in verses 8–9 that Haman's words to the king were very manipulative? He chose his words carefully. He twisted and distorted the perception of what he was actually trying to accomplish, which was to destroy the Jews, avenging a family feud that went back through the family line of Mordecai (from Jacob's bloodline) and Haman (from Esau's bloodline.) In releasing this decree, Haman's plans were revealed for the Jews to see. He overplayed his hand. He revealed his plan.

When Mordecai learned all that had been done, he tore his clothes and put on sackcloth with ashes, and went out into the midst of the city, and cried with a loud and bitter cry.

He went as far as the king's gate because no one was allowed to enter into the king's gate clothed with sackcloth.

In each and every province where the king's command and his decree came there was great mourning among the Jews and fasting, and weeping, and wailing. Many lay in sackcloth and ashes.

So the young women of Esther and her eunuchs came and told her of it. The queen was then seized by anguish. She sent garments to clothe Mordecai so that he could remove his sackcloth, but he would not accept them.

So Esther sent for Hathak, one of the king's eunuchs appointed to attend her and commanded him concerning Mordecai to learn what this was about and why.

[Mordecai told Hathak about all that had happened. Mordecai also gave him a copy of the decree concerning the destruction of the Jews. Hathak returned to Queen Esther and told her all that Mordecai had told him and showed her the decree.]

Esther 4:1–5 (MEV)

Read Esther 4:9–17 in your Bible.

Unless for some reason the king should hold out the golden scepter so that he might live. I, however, have not been summoned to come to the king for these thirty days."

So all the words of Esther were told to Mordecai.

Then Mordecai told them to reply to Esther, "Do not think that in the king's palace you will be more likely to escape than all the other Jews.

For if you remain silent at this time, protection and deliverance for the Jews will be ordained from some other place, but you and your father's house shall be destroyed.

[And who knows if you may have attained royal position for such a time as this?]

Then Esther replied sending back to Mordecai:

"Go gather all the Jews who can be found in Susa, then fast for me. Stop eating and drinking for three days, night or day. I and my young women will fast likewise. Only then would I dare go to the king since it is not allowed by law, and if I perish, I perish."

So Mordecai went away and did exactly as Esther had commanded him.

Esther 4:9–17 (MEV)

What courage! Esther knew she had to take a risk. She came up with a counterattack that was spiritual first: fasting and praying for three days.

Only then would she carry out the second part of the plan. She placed herself in a strategic position before the Lord, and He gave her the strategy.

"On the third day, Esther put on her royal apparel and positioned herself in the king's palace courtyard so that she would be directly in line with the part of the king's throne room where the king sat facing the entrance of the room on his royal throne in the royal hall" (Esther 5:1, MEV).

This put Esther within the king's line of sight. She waited quietly. By being quiet, she held her ground while also respecting the king's authority.

"When the king saw Esther standing [quietly] out in the courtyard, she gained favor in his sight, so the king held out the golden scepter in his hand to Esther. Esther approached and touched the top of the scepter" (Esther 5:2, MEV).

This is a spiritual principle that I have learned. There are times when we war with the Word of God at the enemy. There are also times when we stand silently before our King, Jesus, and gain His favor by staying in His line of sight (staying in a straight line along which the King has an unobstructed view). We don't back up, we don't back down. We simply stand firm. Being quiet allows us to pay attention to the atmosphere around us, both in the spiritual realm and in the physical realm, where we can assess the situation.

We don't move or speak until our King, Jesus, calls for us. We stand or kneel, and we actively listen.

The king responded by offering Esther half the kingdom! Esther invited the king and Haman to a feast that she prepared for him. The king wholeheartedly accepted her invitation and brought Haman along with him. This enabled Esther to gain the higher ground by putting Haman on the defensive. Remember that the devil always overplays his hand. His pride won't permit him to remain quiet. (Haman revealed his whole plan on a decree that he had the king sign, and he sent it all throughout the land, giving God's people the upper hand.)

Read Esther 5:6–14:

> *While drinking wine the king said to Esther, "For whatever you ask, it shall be granted you. So, what is your request? Even if it is for as much as half of the kingdom, it shall be done."*
>
> *Then Esther replied and said, "This is my petition and request. If I have won the king's favor, and if it pleases the king to grant my petition and fulfill my request, then let the king and Haman come to the banquet that I will prepare for them, and tomorrow I will do what the king says."*
>
> *Haman left that day joyfully and with a glad heart, but when Haman saw Mordecai at the king's gate, that he neither stood up or trembled because of him, then Haman was full of indignation against Mordecai.*
>
> *Nevertheless, Haman restrained himself, and when he went to his home he sent for his wife Zeresh and his friends.*

> *Haman recounted to them the glory of his riches, his many children and everything about him the king had praised, and how he had promoted him over the princes and servants of the king.*
>
> *Then Haman continued, "Indeed, Queen Esther brought to the banquet she had prepared, no one but the king and me, and tomorrow I am again invited by her with the king.*
>
> *Yet for all of this, I am not satisfied whenever I see Mordecai the Jew sitting at the king's gate."*
>
> *With this, Haman's wife and friends suggested to him that he should have a gallows built and ask the king in the morning if he could have Mordecai hanged on it. Then go merrily with the king to the banquet.*
>
> *The suggestion pleased Haman so he had the gallows built.*
>
> **Esther 5:6–14 (MEV)**

Haman had a prideful spirit. He opened himself up for judgment by thinking he was more important than he really was. In fact, the spiritual powers at work in Haman were all too happy to play into his inflated opinion of himself.

But God made the king restless, and he could not sleep. The Lord was busy working on behalf of His people, the Jews. Look at Esther 6:1–4:

During that night the king could not sleep, so he ordered that the book of memorable acts be brought, and they were read before the king.

It was found written that Mordecai had informed on Bigthana and Teresh, the two eunuchs of the king serving as the keepers of the door, who had sought to assault King Xerxes.

So the king said, ["What honor or dignity has been done for Mordecai as a result of this?"] Then the king's servants said, "Nothing has been done for him."

So, the king said, "Who is out in the courtyard?" Now Haman had just then entered from across the palace courtyard in order to speak to the king about hanging Mordecai on the gallows that he had prepared for him.

Esther 6:1–4 (MEV)

Note the timing: who did God place in the courtyard but Haman, and why did he enter the courtyard? "To speak to the king about hanging Mordecai."

Watch as God completely turns the table on the plans of the enemy of His chosen people.

The king's attendants said, "Haman is waiting in the court."

> *So the king said, "Let him enter."*
>
> *And Haman entered. Now the king said to him, "What should be done for the man whom the king desires to honor?*
>
> *Haman thought in his heart, "Who more than me would the king desire to honor?"*
>
> *So Haman answered the king, "For the man whom the king delights to honor, let royal apparel be brought that the king himself has worn, and a horse on which the king has ridden, which has a royal insignia on its head.*
>
> *Let the apparel and horse for this man be handled by one of the king's noble officials in order to dress the man whom the king delights to honor, as well as to lead him on horseback throughout the city. And finally, let it be proclaimed before him. "Like this, it shall be done for the man whom the king delights to honor."*
>
> **Esther 6:5–9 (MEV)**

Proverbs 23:7 (NKJV) states, "As a man thinks in his heart so is he: Eat and drink, says he to thee; but his heart is not with thee."

Haman only thought of himself, and his heart was not with anyone but himself. Look at that list of "honors" he came up with, thinking the king was going to honor him. The devil is all too happy to let prideful hearts be led to their own destruction. As it is written in John 10:10 (NIV),

"The thief comes only to steal and kill and destroy; I have come that they may have life, and have it to the full."

It is clear to me that Haman's identity was rooted in who he thought he was and how he appeared before "man." Our identity as children of God is rooted in our Father in heaven and His one and only begotten Son, Jesus, and in the Holy Spirit in us.

In John 17:23 (NIV), Jesus said, "I in them and You in Me—so that they may be brought to complete unity. Then the world will know that you sent me and have loved them even as you have loved me."

"Then the king said to Haman, "Quickly take the apparel and the horse, as you have said, and do so for Mordecai, the Jew sitting at the king's gate. Of everything you have spoken, do not fall short of any of it" (Esther 6:10, MEV).

God set Mordecai up for favor in the midst of his enemies.

Haman did all that the king had decreed. Haman, in true cowardly fashion, ran right to his wife and friends to complain and lament what had just happened.

Listen to what his friends and wife tell Haman in verse 13: "If Mordecai, before whom you have begun to fall, is of Jewish lineage then you will not be victorious over him. Rather, you will surely fall before him" (Esther 6:13, MEV).

As Haman, his wife, and his friends were still talking, one of the king's eunuchs arrived and rushed Haman to the banquet that Esther had prepared.

> *So, the king and Haman entered to feast and drink with Queen Esther. The king repeated to Esther what he had said on the previous day while drinking wine, "For what are you asking, Queen Esther? It shall be granted to you. Now, what is your request?"*
>
> *Queen Esther replied, "If I have found favor in your sight, O king, and if it pleases the king, at my petition, let my life be given me, and my people at my request. For we have been sold, I and my people, to be destroyed, to be slain, and to be annihilated. If only we had been sold as male and female slaves, I could have kept quiet, for that distress would not be sufficient to trouble the king."*
>
> *Then King Xerxes answered and demanded of Queen Esther, "Who is he, and where is he, who would dare presume in his heart to do so?"*
>
> *Esther said, "This wicked Haman is the adversary and the enemy!"*
>
> *Then Haman was seized with terror before the king and queen.*
>
> *[God's enemies are our enemies, and our enemies are God's enemies. But always remember that our fight is not against flesh and blood but against ruling spiritual forces.]*

> *Then the king arose from the banquet of wine in his wrath and went into the palace garden. But Haman remained to plead for his life from Queen Esther, for he saw that harm was determined against him by the king.*
>
> *Now the king returned from the palace garden back to the hall of the banquet as Haman was falling on the couch where Esther was.*
>
> *Then the king said, "Will he also violate the queen while I am in the room?"*
>
> *As the shout erupted from the king's mouth, they covered the face of Haman. Then Harbona, one of the eunuchs in the king's presence, said, "The gallows, fifty cubits high, which Haman had constructed for Mordecai (who had spoken well on behalf of the king), stands at the house of Haman."*
>
> *Then the king said, "Hang him on the gallows that he had prepared for Mordecai." Then the king's wrath was pacified.*
>
> **Esther 7:1–10 (MEV)**

Notice how the Lord's signature is all over this story. Clearly, He wrote and orchestrated into every circumstance His divine plan to save God's people. He used a courageous woman and a courageous man to accomplish His will. This is not where the story ends, though; it goes on to explain how the king reversed the letters that Haman the Agagite had devised, which he wrote in order to destroy the Jews. The king also rewarded Esther and Mordecai by giving them the house of Haman. The king gave Mordecai the place of honor that Haman once held, and Mordecai was given the signet ring of King Xerxes in order that he could write in the king's name on behalf of the Jews and seal it with the king's signet ring.

Because a document written in the king's name and sealed with his signet ring cannot be repealed, Mordecai sent out these letters to all of the kingdoms of Xerxes, and the Jews gained power over those who hated them. The feast of Purim was established. Haman's entire family line was hanged on the same gallows as Haman.

Note: God gave the house and all the belongings to Mordecai and Esther. They were permitted to take over the spiritual territory of those who stood opposed to them.

> *Therefore, the Jews of the rural areas who were living in the villages, made the fourteenth day of the month Adar a day of rejoicing and feasting and a special day for sending portions of food to one another.*
>
> *So Mordecai recorded these events and sent letters to all the Jews throughout all the provinces of King Xerxes, both near and far, in order to institute for them the celebration for the fourteenth day and the fifteenth day of the month of Adar, each and every year like the days when the Jews had rest from their enemies, and like the month when the things turned around for them- Changing from*

> *sorrow to joy....*
>
> **Esther 9:19–22 (MEV)**

Right now, you may be thinking, *That's a great story, but where is the ROAR in this story?*

Look at these verses again:

"When Mordecai learned all that had been done, he tore his clothes and put on sackcloth with ashes, and went out into the midst of the city, and cried with a loud and bitter cry" (Esther 4:1, MEV).

Also, look at Esther's reaction to Mordecai's news of the fate of the Jews.

Read Esther 4:9–17,

> *"[U]nless for some reason the king should hold out the golden scepter so that he might live. I, however, have not been summoned to come to the king for these thirty days."*
>
> *So, all the words of Esther were told to Mordecai.*
>
> *Then Mordecai told them to reply to Esther, ["Do not think that in the king's palace you will be more likely to escape than all the other Jews.*
>
> *For if you remain silent at this time, protection and deliverance for the Jews will be ordained from some other place, but you and your father's house shall be destroyed.*

> *And who knows if you may have attained royal position for such a time as this?"]*
>
> *Then Esther replied sending back to Mordecai:*
>
> *"Go gather all the Jews who can be found in Susa, then fast for me. Stop eating and drinking for three days, night or day. I and my young women will fast likewise. Only then would I dare go to the king since it is not allowed by law, and if I perish, I perish."*
>
> *So Mordecai went away and did exactly as Esther had commanded him.*
>
> **Esther 4:9–17 (MEV)**

Mordecai's *ROAR* is in the form of a grieving spirit. He wept and mourned the fate of his people before the king's gate. Esther's *ROAR* was silent. She simply stood still in the perfect spot. She had determined in her heart to stand before the king, even if it meant she would lose her life!

Esther's divine moment from God came exactly at the right time. There are no accidents or coincidences. God's timing is perfect. Esther acquired a great deal of courage. She was willing to die for her people, "And if I perish, I perish."

Courage can mean risking it all, putting God's purpose above our own. There will be people who will try to talk you out of taking risks for God. They may prefer that you stay complacent because it feels uncomfortable for them when you take a stand for God. But we must follow through!

Great risk for God's name and kingdom will bring great reward to those who will take their stand against the enemy. But it will also cost you. You may lose support from friends and even family members.

Remember this: "If God is for us who can be against us?" (Romans 8:31, NIV).

Let the Lord sort it all out. Continue to love those who stand opposed to you. Remember that your war is not with flesh and blood but with principalities, with powers, against the rulers of the darkness of this world, and against spiritual forces of evil in the heavenly realms (Ephesians 6:12).

Whatever the enemy means to harm you with or how he tries to stop you, God will use to strengthen you and forge you in the fires of adversity until you are a beacon of light shining brightly for the whole world to see! In Genesis 50:20 (NIV), Joseph tells his brothers, "You intended to harm me, but God intended it for good, to accomplish what is now being done, the saving of many lives."

Remember how we looked at the lineage of Mordecai and Haman? How I explained that when we are grafted into the family of Christ, we become part of that royal family line?

Romans 9:24–26 states,

> *Even us whom He has called not from the Jews only, but also from the Gentiles? As indeed He says in Hosea:*

> *"I will call those who were not My people, 'My people,' and her who was not beloved, 'Beloved,' and, "In the place where it was said to them, 'You are not My people,' there they shall be called 'sons of the living God.' "*
>
> **Romans 9:24–26 (MEV)**

When the Lord says, "sons of the living God," He is not emphasizing male over female. He is saying sons as in mankind—man and woman alike.

THE WEDDING RING AND THE SIGNET RING, A PROPHETIC WORD

The wedding ring of the bridegroom to His betrothed, His beloved, His bride, becomes a signet ring on her finger.

The wedding ring symbolizes no beginning and no end, for there is no beginning or end to the deity and diadem of Christ. A diadem is, in simple terms, a crown that is encrusted with jewels. It looks similar to a wedding ring—an unbroken band of gold.

A signet ring is similar in that it symbolizes the power of the one who wears it to release or seal edicts, rulings, and laws.

Ancient kings used signet rings to designate authority, honor, or ownership. A signet contained an emblem unique to the king. Official documents were sealed with a dollop of soft wax impressed with the king's signet, usually kept on a ring on his finger. Such a seal certified the document as genuine, much like a notary public's stamp today. *Example*: "And I saw a mighty angel proclaiming in a loud voice, 'Who is worthy to break the seals and open the scroll?'" (Revelation 5:2, NIV).

We know that the answer to that question is *Jesus*.

"Then one of the elders said to me, 'Do not weep! See, the Lion of the tribe of Judah, the Root of David, has triumphed. He is able to open the scroll and its seven seals'" (Revelation 5:5, NIV).

The Lord Brought Me to the Book of Haggai

Zerubbabel is the governor of the rebuilt Jerusalem and is himself of royal blood, being a descendant of David.

In Haggai's prophecy, God is giving Zerubbabel encouragement and hope. The governor is "chosen" for a unique and noble purpose. As God's signet ring, Zerubbabel is given a place of *honor* and *authority.* God is reinstating the Davidic line and renewing His covenant with David. Judah still has a future as they look forward to the coming Son of David, the Messiah, who would one day "overturn royal thrones and shatter the power of the foreign kingdoms" (Haggai 2:22, NIV).

My Servant, My Signet, My Son

Zerubbabel is also called "my servant." This title was often a Messianic reference in the Old Testament (2 Samuel 3:18; 1 Kings 11:34; Isaiah 42:1–9, 53:12; Ezekiel 34:23–24, 37:24–25). The three represent servant, son, and signet ring, and create a special combination of encouragement given to few in Scripture. Zerubbabel was an important leader involved in the reconstruction of the Jewish temple. As God's "signet ring," Zerubbabel becomes a picture of the future Messiah, Jesus Christ, who will establish His people in the Promised Land, construct an even grander temple (Zechariah 6:12–13), and lead the righteous in never-ending worship (Psalm 49:9).

"Daughters of Kings are among your honored women; at your right hand is the royal bride in gold of [Ophir]" (1 Kings 10:22, NIV).

Jesus's true followers worship the Lord in Spirit and in truth. "Because our innermost man, [our spirit] is eternal" (John 4:24, NIV).

We are His holy ambassadors, called to release into the earthly realm His kingdom.

Here Is What I Heard Him Who Sits on the Throne Say to His Beloved:

"Yes, I will bring My beloved bride her gifts of splendor at the wedding feast of the bridegroom! For, on that day, she will be one holy nation under her King.

I Am her King. Her eternal love. And she shall worship Me in spirit and in truth as I endow her with crowns of splendor and royal jewels of anointing, and rings of My everlasting kingdom, that have My mark upon them as a wedding ring and a signet, which is of her inheritance from My everlasting kingdom. *Fear not!*

I have given you this authority even now! Have I not told you that you would tread upon the serpent and scorpion and not be harmed? Even so, your flesh is not seated with Me yet. Your mind, will, and emotions are still in their carnal form. But I tell you the truth, that your spirit is already seated with Me in heaven.

So carry out My kingdom in the here and now without fear of harm to your flesh. You are yet flesh and bone, but as I have already stated, your spirit is eternal and is already seated in My courts. So pray with power in the Spirit and command the gates of hell to be pushed back. Show My enemies your proof of inheritance—My signet ring. My Spirit has already marked you as Mine. And My blood is the wax that holds My mark upon you.

Now go! Spread My kingdom. For where My Spirit is, there is freedom.

Remember, I came to set the captives free! You have the same power in the Spirit of Truth! He is My deposit in you that you are in Me. You are My bride, forever sealed for My kingdom, and I have given you authority to set the captives free! What are you waiting for?

Freely, I have given to you the keys of the kingdom. Freely give unto others this same hope!

Now Go!"

Amen! *Hallelujah!* Thank You, great and awesome God! You are great and greatly to be praised!

CHAPTER 9:

FINDING YOUR ROAR!

In the first chapter, we looked at the roar of the Lion of Zion. We looked at an actual lion's ROAR. We learned that Jesus wants to restore the roar of His daughters. "The lionesses' ROAR is being restored." We looked at many verses in the Bible that describe the tribe of Judah as a lion or a lioness. We learned that we have been grafted into the family tree of Christ when we became believers and followers of the one true King.

"Then the King will say to those on His right, "Come, you who are blessed by my Father; take your inheritance, the kingdom prepared for you since the creation of the world" (Matthew 25:24, NIV).

We learned that the "shout of the King" is among us. The shout of the King is Jesus's voice of authority, which He has given to His children so that we can overcome the enemies of God (Joshua 6:2–5; Numbers 23:21).

We learned the "spirit cry," which is the ROAR of the Holy Spirit in us (Romans 8:26).

We see that the Lord will stop at nothing to protect His inheritance (*us*) in Deuteronomy 32:9.

We learned about the spiritual battles that are happening all around us and how important it is to understand the armor of God and how to put it on.

We learned that we must wield our weapons of warfare with wisdom and power from the throne room. We need to have an armor check every night before bed and how to raise up hedges of protection over us and our families in Ephesians 6.

We talked in depth about knowing our true identity and how all of what we are and what we accomplish for His kingdom is wrapped up in this knowledge in John 15:9–12.

We also learned how important it is that we guard our doors and gates.

The power of life and death resides in the tongue. We must watch and see what God wants to show us and protect our eyes, ears, and all of our senses from letting Satan find a foothold (James 4).

We learned to be still before the Lord and wait for His instruction in Exodus 14:14, Psalm 46:10, and Psalm 37:7.

In the second chapter, we spent time in the book of Joshua, breaking down some key points in the famous battle for Jericho. We looked at the battle from the eyes of the Lord, from the *prophetic* point of view.

Because Joshua's eyes were opened by the Father to see into the spirit realm from an eagle's point of view, he was able to perceive the spiritual battle that was simultaneously taking place with the physical realm battle. Joshua understood that one realm is as real as the other and that the heavenly realm has greater kingdom significance (Joshua 6:2).

We discussed the Lord's battle strategy in Joshua Chapter 6.

We took a look at the nature of the believer's weapons and how important spiritual preparation is. Listening and obtaining permission from the throne of the Lord is the only way we can go into a territory and take the spiritual atmosphere for the kingdom and for the Lord. Patience, obedience, and endurance are our keys.

We witnessed how Jesus, our King, the Lion of the tribe of Judah, used His kingly authority through the battle cry of His people to tumble those walls!

"Do not let a word come out of your mouth until I say shout, then SHOUT! Shout the battle cry, for the LORD has given you the city!" (Joshua 6).

The Lord, strong and mighty, released His ROAR on the seventh time around the city on the seventh day, and

His ROAR inhabited the battle cry of His beloved people, and the walls came tumbling down!

In Chapters Three and Four, we discovered the reluctant warrior Gideon in the book of Judges on the threshing floor as he hid from his enemies. Then, one day, God showed up, and the angel of the Lord said, "The LORD is with you, O mighty man of valor" (Judges 6:12, NIV).

We watched as Gideon made an offering unto the Lord as a sign of His covenant with Him. The Lord accepted it and sealed an oath between them.

We witnessed Gideon's reluctance cultivated and forged into trust in the Lord, which gave Gideon the courage to tear down the poles and smash the idols that the enemies of Israel had erected to worship their false gods.

Gideon was careful to follow every command that God gave him, just as Joshua had also done.

In Chapter Four, we continued learning from Gideon as we further explored Gideon's exploits for the Lord in Judges 6. In Judges 7, we witnessed God whittle Gideon's mighty army into a group of only 300 men based on how they drank water from the river. The men who kept their heads up showed their awareness of their surroundings.

We saw how Gideon stopped, and he was still, and he listened. Because he listened, Gideon heard a prophecy about himself from the enemy's camp. "This is none other than the sword of the LORD and of Gideon, God has given Midian and the whole camp into his hands" (Judges 7:14, NIV).

This very prophecy came true with the battle cry that the Lord used through His beloved people, as they shouted at the Lord's command, "A sword for the Lord, and for Gideon!"

We see that God always confirms His Word to us. When God says, "Listen or see," He is actually saying so much more!

We saw Gideon stop and worship God and give Him the glory and honor that belongs to Him. We learned that knowing the right time to enforce a strategy in battle is extremely important (Judges 7:15).

In Chapter Five, we looked at Deborah, also from the book of Judges.

The whole of Chapter 5 of Judges is devoted to the song of Deborah. She sang of the Lord as she roared into battle with Barak, son of Abinoam.

Judges 4 explains the many different facets of the mantle Deborah carried: Deborah was a devoted wife and mother. She was a mighty woman of God. She was appointed by God to be a judge and prophet over Israel. She had great compassion and presided over and resolved disputes among the Israelites.

Deborah's calling was to declare God's will to His chosen people and to keep them from going astray.

We learned a little bit about how "powers and dark forces" can set up spiritual strongholds for Satan, fencing in our minds and darkening our understanding so that we do not understand the Word of God (Judges 4:6–10).

We learned that when we wrestle with the Word of God, Jesus, we will end up walking away with a limp, like Jacob in Genesis 32.

We also learned that it is better to walk with a limp that was given in our wrestling with God and learning to submit to His will (*tap out*) than it is to grapple with Satan and end up being destroyed! James 4:7 (NIV) states, "Therefore submit yourselves to God. Resist the devil, and he will flee from you."

We witnessed the same principles at work over and over again.

In Chapter Six, we observed what it means to be a giant slayer.

We looked further into our true identity as children of God and co-heirs with Christ (Galatians 2:19–21). Acts 17:28 (NIV) states: "For in Him, we live and move and have our being. As some of your own poets have said, "we are His offspring."

Colossians 3:12–17 (NIV) shows us that we literally "put on Christ." He is our authority—the deposit of the Holy Spirit within us, and Christ, who is our covering, is who we are! This is also the beginning of understanding the heart of Christ for His beloved (*us*).

The Lion of the tribe of Judah is the authority of Christ. The Lamb that was slain but is risen is the heart of Christ. His desire is for us to have His heart for people, and we must "see" (perceive) through the eyes of His authority.

We talked about how important it is to know when to lean into the Father in worship and when to move forward in battle. That is why God called King David "a man after My own heart." When it comes to giant slayers, David is our role model. We saw the battle strategy from an eagle's point of view, perceiving the big picture, and then we were able to head into battle.

We saw that one of the enemy's favorite tactics is *fear*! (1 Samuel 17:8–11, 14–16). We saw how important it is to pick our fights carefully. The battle is not ours. Victory belongs to the Lord. Fear and offense are the devil's top two tactics. James 1:19–20 (MEV) states, Therefore, my dear brothers, let every man be swift to hear, slow to speak, and slow to anger, for the anger of man does not work the righteousness of God.

In Chapter Seven, we discovered that "we," who are in Christ Jesus, are all firstborn in the sight of the Father.

"I shall make Him my firstborn, the highest of all the kings of the earth. In my mercy, I will keep Him forever, and My covenant shall stand firm with Him" (Psalm 89:27–28, MEV).

We see that firstborn is as much a title as it is a description of birth order. We are all firstborn in Christ Jesus, so we all carry the birthright of victory over our foes. Hallelujah!

This is an excellent and beautiful example of knowing our identity.

"Truly I say to you, whatever you bind on earth will be bound in heaven, and whatever you loose on earth will be loosed in heaven" (Matthew 18:18, MEV).

In Christ, we are considered firstborn, which means that we share in Jesus's inheritance. Being firstborn is positional. We are seated with Christ in heavenly places, in the presence of God, our Father (scriptures referenced: Ephesians 1:20, 2:6). So, when we pray, we are simultaneously praying "on earth as it is in heaven" (Matthew 6:10, NIV). As we agree with our Father, in the name of the Son, we are exerting Christ's authority by the Holy Spirit in us, carrying out His perfect will.

"And He raised us up and seated us together in the heavenly places in Christ Jesus" (Ephesians 2:6, MEV).

We witnessed yet another example of what happens when our "zeal" for the Lord is misunderstood as hubris or pride when David's older brother questioned David's motive for going to the battle's front line. Never let other people's opinions of you penetrate your skin! We have to have a tough hide so that the darts of the enemy will not get through and wound us in our minds, wills, and emotions. Do not let their criticism and attitudes squash your enthusiasm.

God is always looking for those of us who desire to carry out His will from a heart that is surrendered completely to Him. "The LORD looks down from heaven on the children of men, to see if there were any who have insight, who seek God" (Psalm 14:2, Psalm 53:2, MEV).

David pressed into God in the wilderness. He slew a bear and a lion. Those smaller battles were key in teaching David how to fight and grow in his understanding of God's faithfulness. As he won those battles in the wilderness, his trust in God grew, which prepared him for the bigger battles that were ahead of him. Wilderness seasons are necessary for our spiritual growth. Without the valley, we would never appreciate the mountaintop. In the valley or wilderness, we learn to discern the voice of the Father. We learn to trust in and depend on Him.

We saw David properly display righteous anger. He was in right standing with God, and he was angry that "this uncircumcised Philistine should defy the armies of the Almighty God!" (1 Samuel 17:26, NIV). God is always on the side of His justice. Not justice as the world sees it. Justice as was intended from the beginning.

Our battles really are not with people. When we focus our energy fighting with people, we are misguided. Our fight is with Satan and his minions.

David's motive was righteous! He set his heart on the reputation of God and Israel. David saw the battle from a heavenly perspective. He knew that he had already overcome his enemy. He understood that small battles lead to good training for bigger battles. He knew that he was ready to fight for the Lord on this day.

Bigger battles put our trust in God on display. People observe how we handle ourselves as the Lord fights for us. It is a testimony to those who are watching, believers and non-believers alike. "Nevertheless, He saved them for His name's sake, that He might make His mighty power known" (Psalm 106:8, MEV).

We see how comparing ourselves to others and trying to fit into their armor won't work. We are issued our own set of God's armor that is fitted perfectly to us. Saul let David have his armor, but it was too big and cumbersome. David promptly removed it and went into battle equipped with the helmet of salvation, the breastplate of righteousness, and the sword of the Spirit (Ephesians 6:17). Other than that, he carried into battle only his staff, five smooth stones in a bag, and a slingshot (1 Samuel 17:40). David was covered in God's grace. Grace equals power plus favor. The Spirit of the Lord was upon him.

In Chapter Eight, we took a look at Esther and Mordecai. We learned about Esther and Mordecai's lineage and the lineage of Mordecai's archenemy, Haman.

We discovered that this feud went all the way back to Jacob and Esau. Jacob's grandfather and Esau's grandfathers were enemies (Genesis 25:19–34; Romans 9:24–26). We learned that we are a part of Esther and Mordecai's lineage because we are firstborn in Christ, and therefore, we are graphed into the family line of Jesus.

We witnessed Esther listen to Mordecai and watched as she made shrewd choices. She brought only with her what the king's eunuch, Hegai, advised her to bring when she met the king. God's favor rested on Esther, and that caused everyone else to favor her, especially King Xerxes, who made her queen.

We also witnessed God's favor of Mordecai. He positioned Mordecai at the king's gate, where important issues of the kingdom were decided. We discovered that there are spiritual gates over regions ruled by powers and principalities. Unless God's people learn to strategically place ourselves at these strategic areas in our spheres of influence, as Mordecai did, we will end up leaving the territory in enemy hands.

Remember that Mordecai was in the right place at the right time, as a plot was hatched that would have led to the murder of King Xerxes. Mordecai had the wisdom to recognize his opportunity to gain favor for himself in the sight of the king by revealing the plot. We know that God is sovereign and that nothing happens by coincidence. There is no Hebrew word for coincidence. The Hebrew people believe in divine providence. So, Mordecai and Esther were exactly where God wanted them to be.

We witnessed Mordecai, over and over again, refusing to bow to Haman. That made Haman burn with anger. Haman wanted to destroy all of the Jews because of the age-old grudge that he carried. He plotted and schemed, but to no avail. These same spiritual powers that have been over the nations for thousands of years are still in operation today.

We witnessed these spiritual powers at work as Mordecai mourned at the king's gate the decree that Haman manipulated the king into signing so that Haman could have an excuse to destroy God's people.

Esther courageously called for a three-day fast from all of the Jews, knowing that she would have to present herself to the king without him calling for her, which could cost her life. Mordecai's words to Esther are remembered even today, "And who knows if you may have attained royal position for such a time as this?"

Likewise, Esther showed such courage with her reply, "If I perish, I perish" (Esther 4:16, NIV).

She planned a counterattack in the spiritual realm first by calling a fast and drawing near to the Father to summon her courage. Then, she strategically placed herself in the courtyard directly in the king's line of sight. By placing herself in this strategic position in front of the Lord, she showed Him that she was willing to die to try to save His chosen people, and she was willing to face the consequences if her plan failed. The Lord gave her this strategy, and she followed through.

The king saw her standing quietly in the courtyard, all dressed up and looking lovely. We learned from Esther that there is a time when we must stand in our King Jesus's line of sight and remain silent until He tells us to make a move. We hold our ground, we don't back up, and we don't back down.

Esther was shrewd when she invited Haman to a feast with only her and the king. She caught him off balance. Remember that Haman overplayed his hand by putting down his entire plan as a decree, sending it out to everyone in all of the kingdom, and then bragging about how awesome he thought he was. As usual, his pride was his downfall.

God's enemies are our enemies. Again, we see that our fight is not against flesh and blood. It is against ruling spiritual forces that oppose the will of God in our lives.

We saw how God caused the king to be restless and unable to sleep, how one of the king's servants brought the king the exact decree to read about how Mordecai had saved his life by reporting the plot that he witnessed at the king's gate. This led to the king wanting to honor Mordecai, which led to the downfall of Haman. The king ordered that Haman was to be hung by the very gallows he had built to hang Mordecai from.

We witnessed through every plot twist and turn of the enemy how God provided a promise to deal with the problem. God knows Satan better than he knows himself. After all, God created all things. There is not one thing that exists that God did not create. "If God is for us, who can be against us?" (Romans 8:31, MEV).

We see over and over again in every chapter how the enemy overplayed his hand by boasting and bragging. He cannot resist! When he does this, he always ends up revealing his weakness: *pride*. All of our battles come down to Satan and his minions against us and the army of God before us and behind us. Our battles are over before they ever begin.

"I will greatly rejoice in the LORD, my soul shall be joyful in my God; for He has clothed me with garments of salvation, He has covered me with the robe of righteousness, as a bridegroom decks himself with ornaments, and as a bride adorns herself with her jewel's" (Isaiah 61:10, MEV).

So, what does your ROAR sound like? Is it that of a leader of God's people who is confident, who has a ROAR like Joshua's? Is it a reluctant servant-turned-warrior ROAR like Gideon's? Is your ROAR a singing song into battle kind of ROAR like Deborah's? Does your ROAR reflect your confidence in your relationship with God as David's did? Perhaps you have a ROAR of mourning like Mordecai's or a ROAR that was silent but deafening to the enemy, like Esther's. The point is we all have a Holy Spirit-filled ROAR of our own. The Lion of the tribe of Judah is calling His lionesses to ROAR their way to the front lines of battle!

Daughters of God and brides of Christ, it is coronation day!

CORONATION DAY: A PROPHETIC WORD FOR THE BRIDE

This morning, as I was in between my sleeping and waking state, in the quiet of my mind, I began to hear the chime of church bells in a celebratory fashion.

As the bells continued to ring out, in my spirit, I asked the Lord, "What is this that I am hearing?" I heard Him say to me, in the spirit, "It is the sound of heaven celebrating. It is coronation day."

Still, in the spirit, I asked, "What does this mean?" He said to me, "The queen is receiving her crown." I knew in my spirit that He was speaking of Esther.

Esther is symbolic of God's daughters, who are being called forth, "For such a time as this!"

Later that morning, as I walked along a familiar path with my husband and my dog, I noticed that the morning glories were in their full splendor. They had been dormant for a very long time, but suddenly there they were, in their royal purple-blue hue, announcing the coronation of God's daughters: the married, who have been waiting a long time to be used by God for His glory at just the right time, and the unmarried, who are longing to find and fulfill their calling and destiny.

This word brings blessings to those who have fought long and have not wavered. This crosses all generations. For grey is a crown of glory, as is youth!

The young daughters will be known for their courage and strength. The seasoned ones will be known for their strength and wisdom in the Lord!

Their husbands are blessed among the nations because of their humbleness, and they also have a share in victory! For their carts will be filled to overflow, and their houses will be filled with the bounty of the Lord.

So, come forth, daughters of the King, kneel and bring your head low in His presence. He will crown your head and raise you up!

Hallelujah!

"And the word of the LORD is flawless, like silver purified in a crucible, like gold refined seven times" (Psalm 12:6, NIV).

"You crown the year with your bounty, and your carts overflow with abundance" (Psalm 65:11, NIV).

"For the LORD takes delight in his people; He crowns the humble with victory. Let His faithful people rejoice in this honor and sing for joy on their beds" (Psalm 149:4–5, NIV).

"Grey hair is a crown of splendor; it is attained in the way of righteousness" (Proverbs 16:31, NIV).

"The glory of the young is their strength, grey hair the splendor of the old" (Proverbs 20:29, NIV).

PRAYER OF ACTIVATION

Lovely ones, I encourage you to take some time and reflect on where He is calling you. When you are ready, I encourage you to pray this prayer with me:

Dear heavenly Father, I kneel at the foot of Your throne. I surrender all of me, for all of Jesus. Jesus, My King, I am ready to suit up in my armor and pick up my weapons of warfare. Open my eyes and ears to things unseen and unknown. Open my eyes to the battles raging around me and my family and go before me into the deep waters. I will follow where You go. When You say stand, I will stand firm. When You say lean in, I will retreat to Your side. I turn my face toward You on Your throne, and I await my commissioning.

In the name of Jesus Christ, the Lamb who was slain and is risen, and in the name of Jesus, the Lion of the tribe of Judah, I declare over Your daughters that this is the day of their coronation. They are commissioned and have begun the journey to becoming equipped for battle. I declare activation of the heart of the King of kings in the women who read this book. Lord, let Your kingdom come now into the hearts of the courageous ones who answer the call to arms. Forever, Lord, let Your will be done in their hearts, homes, and dominions. In Jesus's mighty name.

Let the name of King Jesus be written on their shields

of faith. Let the Lord call them forth by name. Let Your banner of love be raised over them.

And now, if you receive this commission, come forward and *ROAR!*

I encourage you who have taken up your place in the battle to pursue other books and teachings on spiritual warfare so that you may be more fully equipped.

In His Love,

L. M. Hernandez

BIBLIOGRAPHY

Bevere, Lisa. *Girls With Swords: How to Carry Your Cross Like a Hero*. Colorado: WaterBrook Press, 2013

Bible Study Tools. "Deborah." Accessed October 26, 2023. https://www.biblestudytools.com/dictionary/deborah/

Brewer, Troy. *Numbers That Preach.* California: Aventine Press, 2007

Jacobs, Cindy. *Possessing the Gates of the Enemy: A Training Manual for Militant Intercession.* Michigan: Baker Publishing Group, 2009

Prince, Derek. *Spiritual Warfare for the End Times: How to Defeat the Enemy*. Michigan: Baker Publishing Group, 2017

Rose Publishing. *Names of God.* Peabody, Massachusetts: Rose Publishing, 2018

Shirer, Priscilla. *The Armor of God.* Tennessee: LifeWay, 2015

Trimm, Cindy. *The Rules of Engagement: The Art of Strategic Prayer and Spiritual Warfare*. Florida: Creation House, 2005

Printed in the USA
CPSIA information can be obtained
at www.ICGtesting.com
LVHW010221210224
772321LV00014B/537